(Continued from front flap)

ing of Christian conduct, and the use of existential methods. An unusually extensive bibliography provides a rich mine for further reading in these fields.

Written for ministers, directors of Christian education, members of Christian education committees, workers in the local church school, and for use in college and seminary classes, this book will also be of vital interest to parents and others concerned for a truly dynamic program of Christian nurture.

DR. IRIS V. CULLY studied at Adelphi College (A.B.); Hartford Seminary Foundation (A.M.); Garrett Biblical Institute (B.D.); and Northwestern University (Ph.D.). Director of Religious Education at Hollis, Long Island, New York, Presbyterian Church from 1937 to 1939, she then married the Rev. Dr. Kendig Brubaker Cully, now Professor of Religious Education at Seabury-Western Theological Seminary. They have lived in Evanston, Illinois, since 1951. Dr. Cully has written curriculum materials for the Presbyterian Church U.S.A, the Congregational Christian Churches, the Evangelical and Reformed Church, and The Methodist Church, and has contributed widely to religious journals. She has taught at Baptist Missionary Training School, Chicago, at Garrett Biblical Institute (where she is in charge of the curriculum laboratory), at Northwestern University, in leadership training schools and conferences, and in her home parish. The Cullys, with their two teen-age daughters, spent seven months in 1956 touring Europe and Great Britain, where they studied religious education in the churches of many countries. A previous book by Dr. Cully, co-authored by her husband, is *Two Seasons: Advent and Lent*.

The Dynamics
of
Christian Education

The Dynamics
of
Christian Education

by

IRIS V. CULLY

The Westminster Press: PHILADELPHIA

To

My Husband,

Kenne Japanese Christy

"There is no fear in love; but perfect love casts out fear." (1 John 4:18)

Contents

Contents

Preface

Those persons responsible for Christian nurture are showing concern that children's lives shall be rooted in the fellowship of the church, that their faith shall be awakened by the hearing of the gospel, and that their lives shall be guided by the work of the Holy Spirit. For these reasons, contemporary understandings in Biblical study and in Biblical theology are finding a response among workers in the field of religious education. Many are seeking ways by which understandings of the Christan faith that have been meaningful to believers since the earliest days of the church can be meaningful in the lives of growing persons now. They are certain that God still speaks through the pages of Scripture, and they hope that he will so speak to boys and girls and young people today. They know that the church is a fellowship different from any other group among which people seek companionship, and they hope that today's children will sense the difference, being drawn to seek the completion of their individual lives within the life of this redemptive community.

The *kērygma,* the proclamation of the good news that in Jesus Christ God has entered human existence, seeking and saving men, is the very heart of the Christian faith. This is the message around which the life of the church is oriented and which it bears to all the world. The following chapters seek to interpret the relevance of the proclamation for the work of Christian nurture. It is hoped that thereby a groundwork may be laid for experimental teaching and writing by many people across the coming years.

The first chapter sets the educational tasks of the church and school side by side, concluding that the church has specific functions which need to be kept clearly in mind when developing the content and methodology for communicating the faith.

Contemporary thinking concerning the nature of the church and the essential content of the message are next explored. An appreciable consensus is observed among the exponents of what might be termed an ecumenical theology, concerning the church as a living fellowship and the message as the good news of God's redeeming love shown to mankind in Jesus Christ. This is the foundation for the church's teaching.

A parallel survey of contemporary literary, philosophical, and psychological thought suggests that persons today are anxious and insecure, seeking love and acceptance. It is evident that even little children have this need. The " good news " is meant for such as these.

The subject of communication is next explored. The ways of meeting between God and man are set forth, as well as avenues of understanding among persons.

Through Chapter 4 the book leads to the following conclusion: the dynamic Biblical theology being enunciated today, the present understanding of the nature and needs of persons, and the newer explorations into the subject of communication make necessary the development of somewhat different methods from those which were previously satisfactory for conveying religious insights.

Subsequently, life-centered methods are suggested through which this dynamic understanding of the Christian faith can be made meaningful to the lives of children within the context of the church. These methods are set forth as participation, recognition, and communication.

An application of these findings is then made in terms of five areas in which they have relevance for the development of the curriculum for the church school: the church, the Bible, the relationship between God and persons, the understanding of Christian conduct, and the use of existential methods.

The purpose of the present work is to elucidate an understanding of the Christian faith that can be relevant to growing children within the church, to develop methods by which this faith can be communicated to children and by them, and to point to ways in which future curricular materials might incorporate such insights.

The influence of many people within one's personal history goes into the making of a book. Here I would acknowledge especially the help of several persons who have shared many insights with me: Dr. Viola Theman in the field of child development; Dr. William F. Case in the area of group dynamics; Dr. Frank M. McKibben in religious education; and Dr. David C. Shipley, who was for me an illuminating guide into the historical understanding of the gospel.

In the late hours of work, the painstaking checking of sources, and the tedium of corrections, I was upheld by my husband, who not only helped in these pedestrian tasks but gave companionship to our children and strengthened me with his ever-encouraging love.

IRIS V. CULLY

Evanston, Illinois

The School and the Church

THE SCOPE OF EDUCATION

In order to comprehend the meaning of education, we must see it in its full scope. Sensitive educators are aware that the accumulated knowledge and experience of mankind are not the only ingredients of their nurture of the young. They must also bring to their task an understanding of the factors in interpersonal relationships. Psychological findings indicate that growth and development include the whole person within his total environment. Great teachers in the schools have always been aware of such factors operative in their work, but only in the present century have these been spelled out in detail.

The church's educational leaders have shared this increasing concern of their secular colleagues. Precisely because cultural education has spread its field so broadly, those persons concerned with the educational task of the church need to attempt an understanding of the church's unique witness. If there are places where the teaching tasks of the cultural school and the church seem to overlap, it may be that each has a different emphasis, or it may be that one or the other is not fully aware of having a particular responsibility.

Penetrating and extensive thinking is being done today, among both educators and those concerned with theological method. Although the theologians' work is not addressed directly to the church school, a question these writers are asking is pertinent:

What is the essential message of the faith, and how is it communicated?

The school also is examining its "message" and the way of communication. Because Christian children spend five days a week in their communities' schools, the task of the church can be seen from a fresh viewpoint if looked at in relationship to this other important part of cultural life.

THE CONTEXT FOR EDUCATION

The school is the environment in which the young of each generation are taught what the culture desires and demands. The American school is made by the community and is responsible to it. All cultures have established schools in some form and given them particular functions to perform for their children. The learning deemed desirable differs according to the needs of a society and it changes across the centuries, although change within a decade or even a quarter century may be so slow as to seem imperceptible. The American school derives its existence from the community, grows out of the necessity of the community, and has the consent of the community. The type of "community" may vary. In the contemporary pattern, the school is largely controlled by the local municipality or township, while the state sets up minimum standards. Hence it may be said that the school draws its "fellowship" from the community within which it acts. At the same time, the school helps to develop patterns of community thought even while it expresses the current pattern of a civilization.

The school draws the whole quality of its life from this human community. When the community life is full and vital, the schools will be alive. Where a society is weak and poverty-stricken, the schools will be correspondingly restricted. The needs and desires, hopes and fears, tensions and affirmations of a people are to be found in their schools. Where the schools are thus faithful to this community concern, they are preparing children to participate in its life. Methods and materials will be developed toward that end.

The church too is a community. In the contemporary American scene it does not comprise the geographical and sociological community (the parish). The members of the church live in the cultural community, but have a special relationship within the church. They are bound together by a common loyalty and a common purpose, and they desire their children to participate in this life. They feel a responsibility to develop a nurture in accordance with a particular need. They have a function to perform that cannot be done by an outsider.

Only the people within a community can be aware of the community's deeper meanings and be able to express them in terms that will be relevant to the needs of the whole community in its relationships with the past and the present, and its responsibilities to the future. Members have a point of reference from which to select both the methods and the content for education. Just as the cultural educational media for the children of Jonesville, U.S.A., could hardly be selected with any accuracy by a citizen of Mozambique (or even by a citizen from Jonesville of two centuries ago), so the bases for Christian education are necessarily determined by the responsibility of those to whom the church is real and loved. The church begins as a community *within,* yet distinct *from,* the sociological community. " For where two or three are gathered in my name, there am I in the midst of them." (Matt. 18:20.) Their coming together expresses their relationship in Christ with one another. Their fellowship grows out of that awareness. This was the status of the early church within the Roman Empire. This is the situation of Christians in a non-Christian environment. These people have been set apart by their baptism into a new life in Christ, and they want their children to know the fullness of that life. They feel a need to witness to what God has done for them, and they find strength for such testimony in the fellowship of the community. The church has been, from the very beginning, a teaching community.

Wherever and whenever the church is this kind of community, the cultural school does not cause any conflict of loyalties through its community outreach. In whatever way school and society may interact in the development of culture, there is little possibility of invading the religious life of a Christian community. The intrusion more often has been through some form of persecution.

Here, then, are two contexts for education: the cultural community and the community of the church. The latter is contained geographically within the former. A person may belong to the community without participating in the life of the church; but as a member of the church he is also a member of the community. People bring their cultural heritage into the church and thus influence it, sometimes beneficially, and sometimes to the detriment of the specific witness. Members of the church bear testimony in the community to their life in Christ. Sometimes this witness has encouraged community values, sometimes it has involved a sharp criticism of the community; hence the emphasis on the necessity for those who think through the message of the church in contemporary terms to be participants in the worshiping community. For determining both the content and the methodology of Christian education it is needful to keep in mind the distinctive functions of the church toward its people and its responsible witness within the life of the broader community.

THE CENTER OF THE EDUCATIONAL PROCESS

Any educational philosophy has a center. The center around which contemporary cultural education revolves is man.[1] This is a necessary focus in a humanistic society and is in line with the great tradition which, having its classical roots in Greece, entered the modern world through the Renaissance, inspiring great learning, both in the arts and in the sciences. The anthropocentric approach sees in man the source of his own freedom. The root of freedom tends to be thought of as an intellectual freedom, the freedom to think as one chooses and to follow the leadings of such thought.

The writings of Massachusetts' famous nineteenth-century educator Horace Mann indicate that when education became a function of the state, there was no intent to set the schools against religious teaching. The omission of such teaching was done in the interest of removing the schools from religious controversy and of ensuring to every child the right to an elementary education. Increasingly, however, the avoidance of religion resulted in the substitution of moral and ethical teaching (e.g., the McGuffey *Readers*). Man became the center of the educational process, which tended to stress his development and eventually his glorification. This trend reached a zenith in the writings and teachings of a series of great teachers at Columbia University's Teachers College, and was echoed by their graduates in positions of influence throughout the country. John Dewey was the father of this philosophical movement. The point of view more recently has been set forth in books by his successor, William Heard Kilpatrick, and by George S. Counts.

Eventually this can lead to a religion of Man.[2] One writer, finally, questions traditional religion by saying:

> "Religion as a structure of special doctrine has often inhibited the development of religious quality of life and experience. Its tendency to focus man's attention upon an unknowable supernatural world has diverted his energies from the task of improving the quality of actual life and existence." [3]

Although this is an exaggerated outcome of faith in man, nevertheless there seems to be a tendency in the anthropocentric approach to dismiss what is frequently referred to as " supernaturalism." This need not becloud the fact that modern educators have been upholders of a great tradition and have held steadily to the assurance that man is capable of achievements that do honor to his status among created beings.

The church too has a center around which life revolves. This center is God. " Theology," the very title by which its science is called, denotes that fact. Scholarly works in the field of systematic theology invariably begin with an elucidation of the meaning of God within the Christian faith, whether they be from the pen of John Calvin writing in the sixteenth century or Karl Barth writing in the twentieth century. Only when the church knows what it understands about God is it capable of theologizing toward an understanding of man. For in Christian thinking, God is man's creator, the source of his present life, and his ultimate hope. The Christian sees the world as God's gift. He understands Jesus as God's Son. He knows the Bible as the Word through which God makes himself known to man. He can say in all sincerity that "man's chief end is to glorify God, and to enjoy him forever." In this focus, man is important because of his relationship with God.

> "What is man that thou art mindful of him,
>   and the son of man that thou dost care for him?
> Yet thou hast made him little less than God,
>   and dost crown him with glory and honor."
>   (Ps. 8:4-5.)

At the same time man sees himself in the perspective of the eternal God and thereby is saved from imagining that man *is* God. Self-assurance may lead to real achievement, just as work done for the glory of God also may lead to achievement (the cathedrals of the Middle Ages or the music of Johann Sebastian Bach, for instance). But even as men have sometimes done evil to their fellow men in the name of God, so the elevation of man to a quasi-divine status may be a factor in twentieth-century despotisms. The pre-eminence of God was the insight that led early Christians to refuse to burn the pinch of incense before Caesar's statue, as it has kept modern Christians from participation in the patriotic-religious celebrations fostered by some Governments of the present century.

Within the Christian context, it is affirmed that a man finds his fullest freedom through relating himself to God. Freedom implies the ability to choose. The person thus confronted by God may choose relationship to him or may choose to live without him. Each choice has its own consequences.

Thus within the educational contexts there are two centers. Cultural education is anthropocentric; the education of the church is theocentric. Yet each has a witness to make to the other. Cultural education reminds men of their value as human beings and of their potential accomplishments. It will stress the enrichment made by science and aesthetics in those times when some people within the church fail to appreciate these gifts to mankind. The church, by acknowledging God as the center of all existence, can keep men from the distortion of life that comes when they make themselves as gods. Moreover, whereas humanism may overstress the intellectual aspects of life, the church, by affirming that man is not saved by intellect alone but that the whole person is called by God and responds to him, is enabled to denote the worth of each person, made in the image of God. Whereas " man " may become an abstraction, the Biblical " O Lord, thou hast searched me and known me! " (Ps. 139:1) is always a call to particularity.

The danger is that Man with a capital " M," in becoming the center of life, may cease to be a person and become instead an ideal, or a principle. One thinks of the character in Jean-Paul Sartre's novel *Nausea,* who loved Humanity with a great love (so he said) but could not enjoy people. Contrast this with the Christian existentialism of Paul Geren:

" Gauhati, Assam, June 6, 1942
" Today we had to move the evacuee patients out of one hospital building into another. . . . The American turned to his British comrade and said, ' I am very glad at this moment that I am an agnostic.'
" I do not know how seriously he intended this. However that is, the conclusion which he implied certainly held: since he did not believe in the love of Christ he could leave the handling of these dysentery victims to the sweepers. Since his friend did believe in it, he was not free to stand by and watch. Nor was I. Get down in it! Pick the patients up! Soil yourself with this disease! . . . There is no need to call this filthiness sweet, nor to start enjoying it through a strange inversion. Only one thing is necessary: for love's sake it must be done." [4]

These are the distinctions and the emphases that the church needs to keep in mind in thinking through a clear-cut content and methodology for education.

THE NORM FOR THE EDUCATIONAL PROCESS

The norm [5] gives a point of reference by which to select both curriculum and methodology for teaching. The cultural school, set within the framework of the community, is established to help children grow in the understanding of and the desire to participate in the way of life that is deemed most good and true. In the United States this means becoming citizens of a democratic state. Democracy is a concept of an ideal as well as a working form of government. The educators have found it necessary to define this ideal for themselves as they strive for an educational system that embodies it.

The classical book on this subject is John Dewey's *Democracy and Education,* published in 1916. Professor Dewey gives criteria for the democratic ideal:

> " The two points selected by which to measure the worth of a form of social life are the extent in which the interests of a group are shared by all its members and the fullness and freedom with which it interacts with other groups. . . . A society which makes provision for participation in its good for all its members on equal terms and which secures flexible readjustment of its institutions through interaction of the different forms of associated life is in so far democratic. Such a society must have a type of education which gives individuals a personal interest in social relationships and control, and the habits of mind which secure social changes without introducing disorder." [6]

Democracy is seen primarily in its social aspects, and it is understood that the form of government develops as a way of expressing and conserving this way of life.

The historical rootage for the contemporary educational understanding of the concept " democracy " may be found in ancient Greece, particularly in the thought of Plato. This may account for the weight placed on thinking, even on intelligence, in the preparation of persons for participation in the life of a democracy. Actually, Greece never grew beyond a series of city-states, none of which was democratic in the American sense. These city-states were built on a social pyramid resting on a base of slave labor.

It would be illuminating to inquire into democratic rootage from another source: namely, the early Hebrews, who were noted for their rejection of despotism. Abraham led his family out of the city of Ur, and established a tribal pattern under a covenant with Jahweh, their God. Moses led his people out of Egyptian slavery, and during forty years of wilderness living helped them to understand the implications of the covenant made with God at Mt. Sinai. The law was not a yoke imposed by man, but the gracious gift of God, of which a psalmist would write: " Oh, how I love thy law! It is my meditation all the day " (Ps. 119:97).

When the tribes were resettled in the Land of Canaan, they chose judges as their rulers — not as lawmakers, for the law already had been given by God. Later, they demanded a king such as their neighbors had, but the king was anointed — a sign that he was God's chosen one. Moreover, the people reserved the right to reject an unworthy king. They gave an ultimatum to Rehoboam, the son of Solomon; and when he refused it, most of Israel joined Jeroboam in setting up a new kingdom, Judah alone remaining faithful to the house of David.

The prophets condemned injustice as unfaithfulness to God, with whom the people of Israel were bound through the covenant as a man and a woman are joined in marriage. These men stood before kings in the name of the Lord. They cried out against the rich and the powerful. The prophets warned the people whenever fear drove the nation to make compacts with other nations, thus forsaking trust in God.

Determined to be free, the Hebrew people, led by the sons of Maccabee, fought off the Greeks. Finally, they rose up against the power of Rome, and were again dispersed among the nations, taking with them their assurance of being in a special relationship to God, made known in the keeping of the law which he had given them.

The covenantal heritage inspired Calvinistic settlements in

Europe during the first centuries of the Reformation. It influenced the writing of the English bill of rights in 1689, when the Puritans showed their determination that a restored monarchy should not take hard-won freedoms from the people. The idea of the covenant was basic to the seventeenth-century New England settlements, as indicated in such well-known documents as the Mayflower Compact and the Cambridge Platform. A sturdy insistence on the rights of individuals as persons created by God and responsible to him was the contribution of Calvinists to the development of federal government, including the writing of the Constitution of the United States.

The modern flowering of the democratic ideal is traced correctly by the educators through the eighteenth-century Enlightenment in France and the empirical and utilitarian movements in England. In this country, the ideal was enunciated by Benjamin Franklin and Thomas Jefferson, among others.

The relationship between Protestantism and the rise of popular education has not received definitive exposition. Martin Luther saw that people would never fully know the Bible unless each person could read it for himself. This led him to write on the necessity for sending children to school, but the unrest of the times, continued through the hundred years of sporadic religious wars, left this merely a plea. John Calvin began the establishment of schools for elementary education during his years of influence in Geneva. The Presbyterians in Scotland were the first to introduce general education into the British Isles. John Amos Comenius (1592–1670), bishop of the Moravian Brethren, advocated an advanced methodology of a type scarcely used until the nineteenth century.

Popular education first took root in the Western Hemisphere through the New England colonies, where schools early were provided for all children and where the minister was sometimes both pastor and teacher. The Presbyterian minister still bears the title "teaching elder," which also was applied to his Congregational counterpart in colonial days.

Several implications stem from the democratic norm in education. One is that democracy is assumed to be the basis for a belief in the worth of persons. John L. Childs writes, " The morality of democracy . . . is grounded in this principle of the dignity and worth of each human being." [7] Democracy becomes the basis for moral values. Occasionally the imperative for cultural education seems to carry implications that might make an important point of view into an absolute value. J. Paul Williams goes so far as to cite as an " essential religious function of the public schools" what he calls " the teaching of democracy as religion." [8]

This is certainly a radical statement of the secular ideal in education. It is not the first time in history, however, that the norms of a cultural system have been set in opposition to a Biblical point of view. The Greeks tried to Hellenize the Jews. The result was the struggle of the Maccabees. The Book of Daniel mirrors this conflict through the person who chose to enter the den of lions rather than substitute petition to the king for the worship of God. Christians in the early centuries sometimes found that they could not send their children to pagan schools because of the point of view expressed through literature and philosophy.

Christian education accepts the norm of American culture, but cannot regard this in an absolute light. Democracy is part of the Biblical heritage and stems from man's relationship to God, who created him in freedom. But the norm for Christian education is God himself, made known in Jesus Christ. The good news that God has redeemed his people through the Person and work of Jesus Christ, his Son, has been the central affirmation of Christians throughout the centuries. It is therefore to be expected that the content and method for Christian nurture should be found in relation to him. The church's norm is found in a historical Person, who is alike the present head and the hope for time and eternity. He is an objective norm, for his existence is more than the formulation of men's minds. His life is witnessed to through the writings of the New Testament, which are historically as reliable as many other records from that period. He is the norm for man's understanding of God. His life is one of obedience to God. His death shows men how far God will go to draw them to himself. His resurrection is the affirmation of God's triumph over sin and evil. His ascension is the pledge of his eternal reign. The gift of his Spirit is the assurance that he is always with his people. However the understanding of Christ may vary in each generation, there is always a source in the New Testament accounts from which to see him anew. He is not the product of men's hopes, nor the development of their thinking. He is the gift of God and the manifestation of God in human history. He is a concrete norm, yet in his objective character he is outside the immediate situation and so affords both perspective and direction.

Here are two norms for education. Cultural education seeks to help people grow toward what a society conceives to be the balance between individual liberty and corporate existence. This is important, for except as men learn how to live together in smaller communities, it seems unlikely that they will learn how to get along in any world community. But the very ardor with which the people of a nation believe in their ideal and work for its more perfect realization may lead to its becoming an idol. The state could become an absolute; it could become the ultimate point of reference. The democratic state could be seen as the personification of Man, who, as has been noted, tends to be the central focus in the concern of cultural education.

Cultural education reminds Christians that their lives are lived within a total secular community, and that they have a loyalty therein. This was assumed by Paul and made explicit by Martin Luther. The Christian community, by the witness of the members, reminds the state of its limitations. They can guard democracy, admittedly the highest ideal for group living yet developed, against becoming a religion. The existence of the Christian community as a part of the cultural community may act as a leaven to enrich and strengthen democratic ideals; but where the latter threaten to replace the Christian norm of God, made known in Jesus Christ, this smaller community may hold the structure of society in a necessary balance. Democracy could itself become authoritarian. The community of believers always feels the necessity to hold the man-made systems in which all participate before the perspective of the eternal God: to see national history in the light of holy history, and national destiny in the light of God's eternal purposes. This function it can perform among men only while its members are themselves in a deep and true relationship to their norm, even Jesus Christ, the Lord — in short, when they are the worshiping community.

THE CONCEPTUAL BASIS ON WHICH EDUCATION RESTS

An educational system needs a conceptual basis on which to rest, in order that its ideals may have some possibility of realization. The basis for cultural education today lies in the concept of moral and spiritual values. Educators are consistent in affirming that this is the base from which democracy as a way of life can be kept effective. Democracy rests on the quality of the lives of a people, and the phrase "moral and spiritual values" describes the character that is needed in such lives. These values have been generally known as "the true, the beautiful, and the good." They usually include the principle of the Golden Rule. Their authority rests on the pragmatic sanction of social necessity. John S. Brubacher states, "If these things can be seen as inherently true, true to natural human insight, the probabilities seem to us the more promising that under proper guidance youth will accept them to live them." [9]

New psychological insights suggest the possibility that there are inner sanctions for moral conduct. The child who feels loved and who accepts himself does not feel a need to cheat, nor does he feel a need to take credit for not cheating. [10]

A society rests on the quality of its moral and spiritual foundations. The tenor of thinking among many leading present-day American educators is that because of the dynamic nature of the democratic way of life, it is necessary to test the ethical standards that have come down to Western culture, in order that new standards may emerge that will make for a more perfect realization of social and individual good.

The community of the church has a basis on which its education has always rested: the Bible. The cry of the Reformation, first enunciated by Martin Luther, still sounds in the Articles of Religion: "Holy Scripture containeth all things necessary to salvation." This is a specific word. It does not ask the Scriptures to be authoritative for any purpose for which they were not written, and it insists that the believer shall not be required to seek in sources outside the Scriptures for that through which he may be saved.

The Bible is a written word in a historical book. It does not address itself to mankind in general, but to men in particular. It does not speak of "timeless principles," but gives the specific commands of the living God. The prophets addressed their own people. The Gospels recount the actions of a Man living among other men. Paul wrote his letters in answer to questions through which the churches were asking his help.

God is the center of the Biblical record. The writers of the Bible saw his holy purposes in all events. Any attempt to tell a Biblical story without reference to God does violence to the text. Yet, although God made himself known in historical activity, the Bible might conceivably still be only of archaeological and sociological interest. The Bible can be the base for a living faith because God still speaks through it. When a person is stirred to social action because of the words, "Thus says the Lord: . . . Let justice roll down like waters, and righteousness like an ever-flowing stream" (Amos 3:12; 5:24), or when a person faces a life crisis with assurance because he has read, "I will not fail you or forsake you" (Josh. 1:5), then the Word of God is speaking to him. There will be misunderstandings, for the writers were human, and interpreters through the centuries have been equally human. But it may be said justly that there is less distortion when this word is understood within the context of the worshiping community, for the context, as well as the theocentric viewpoint and the norm in Christ, helps to bring it into the focus from which it was originally written. The Biblical writers were men of faith within the covenanted community of Judaism or the community of the church.

The centrality of the Biblical norm has been expressed by contemporary writers in the field of theological method.[11] This norm which guides the church in the educational task has stability because it is grounded in historical events, yet it is made contemporary because it contains the word of the living God. It will be relevant to individual needs and to the problems of men within society because it was written with reference to particular situations and yet is interpreted freshly in each generation.

The Bible has such vitality that a secular society still derives its principal values from those words. The Scriptures have such contemporaneity that they evoke the vision toward which a people press and the ideals for which they yearn. The degree to which a secular society prizes the Bible's teachings and quotes its phrases should bring Christians to face the reality of its demands if at any time they are tempted to glory only in its gifts.

At the same time, the Christian community has in the Bible a treasure which those who develop cultural education necessarily lack. Many of the discussions of moral and spiritual values are arid and abstract reading. In their present form they are reminiscent of Sunday school stories of a moralistic type in which Johnny was naughty; Johnny discovered that it did not pay to be naughty; Johnny resolved to be good. The church has vital stories for children, for the Bible is a record of the lives of people. It is easy to identify with the characters, because they face essentially the same problems that people face today and they make similar mistakes. Human beings are not expected to be like God; they are expected only to love and serve him. This sympathetic attitude toward the frailties of men is a part of the witness of the church to the cultural society. Such an attitude can serve to modify the cultural society's ceaseless striving after the abstract ideal. Objects can be forced into almost any form a human being chooses to give them, but persons will not thus readily conform. To attempt to make them do so and to judge them for their imperfection is to treat persons as objects. This produces a certain hardness and lack of feeling for one another. Instead of promoting the good of each and all, this can arouse hostilities. "Respect for human personality" can be a cold thing. The Bible as the basis for teaching suggests warmth, love, and understanding, for the Bible speaks primarily of God who in Jesus Christ showed himself in love: in the towns of ancient Galilee, on the cross at Calvary, at the supper in Emmaus. "The Word became flesh and dwelt among us" (John 1:14), and this living Word gives the uniquely vital character to the teaching from the Bible.

An ideal can be merely an "it," an abstraction. Human beings are not made to love a *thing,* and when they are confronted with an abstraction as an object of loyalty, they cast about for ways to personalize it. Usually this takes the form of identifying the ideal or value with a person who upholds it or who seems to embody it in his life. This is a potential source of demagoguery, or dictatorship, or of cults in any field of human endeavor. In Christian faith there can be only one Lord; thus the person or object that seeks to take his place in the loyalty of men thereby becomes an embodiment of antichrist. Because Christians have a loyalty to the person of Jesus Christ, through whom the living God has become incarnate in human life, they are in less danger of deifying principles or other human beings. For this reason they can lessen that danger in their culture, offering to the culture the only true focus for loyalty, even God himself.

THE PURPOSE OF EDUCATION

The overarching purpose of cultural education is to fit children for life within the community and the nation. In recent years it has become recognized that a person's ability to respond to the surrounding culture depends on how he has matured personally, in his capacity to accept himself and to be accepted by others. All such personal learning takes place within a group context, whether the family, the neighborhood, or the school.

The Educational Policies Commission, of the National Education Association and the American Association of School Administrators, has set up four areas of objectives for education: self-realization, human relationship, economic efficiency, and civic responsibility. These are the areas that seem important within a democratic framework of living. In the Commission's publication *The Purposes of Education in American Democracy,* the writers say that education is the key to abundant life. It can help the learner understand what constitutes real happiness and make more probable its realization.[12]

This gives a summary of the ways in which a person needs to develop if he is to live as a responsible adult. Self-realization includes the fullest growth in individual potentialities, so that a child may one day find his place in the world vocationally and make a positive contribution to the community. Human relationship is a recognition that no one lives unto himself and that the ability to think of the needs of others is a part of maturity. Getting along with others and concern for others are both a part of this aim. Economic efficiency has a specific connotation regarding work. It suggests that the person has a responsibility toward society to choose the job at which he can be most productive. Civic responsibility involves an understanding of the ideals and purposes of democracy and an effort to realize them in one's society. All of this adds up to what William Heard Kilpatrick calls "the life good to live."[13] These, then, may be stated as the purposes of education: self-realization; the development of satisfying relationships with other people; the use of one's full powers in work; and the acceptance of civic responsibility. Such purposes of education lie within the self and the society. The individual is to be helped to achieve his finest development and to grow in appreciative relations with other persons in order that he may be the kind of citizen who can participate in and further refine the democratic way of life.

The purposes of community education grow out of affirmations about man, democracy, and moral values. The purposes of Christian education grow out of affirmations about God made known through Christ in the Bible. The work of Christian nurture is to explain this good news of God's love in Christ in such a way that those who were born into the faith will know this in their own lives, and those who have responded in faith may understand. The purpose of Christian nurture is to help people through their growing relationship to God in Christ so to live that they may glorify him and effectively serve others, in the assurance that they partake of eternal life now and forever.

Christian nurture sees persons in their relationship to God, who not only seeks man, but has done something to draw men to himself. This "something" is God's saving work through Jesus Christ, proclaimed in the gospel message. This message is a form of testimony by which persons within the community proclaim to others what God has done for them and is doing in and through them by the Holy Spirit for the redemption of the whole world. This is a witness of changed lives and self-fulfillment through a new relationship to God in Christ. It can be made only by persons who have had the experience, from the earliest disciples to those of the present day.

The reason why this kind of personal proclamation should be among the purposes of the church is the fact that persons respond to other persons. The one who witnesses says, in effect: "I know how you feel and what you need, for I too have feelings and needs. This is what God does for me; this is what he offers to you." The gospel offers the fullest development of individual potentialities, but it says that this can come about only as a person assesses his present situation in the light of the holy love of God as it was shown in the living, dying, rising Jesus. What results from this is a transformed life; "eternal life," the Fourth Gospel calls it. This kind of living is made possible by the immanent Holy Spirit. "Salvation" is not an abstract concept. It is God's continuing activity in response to man's deepest human need. It is not a thing apart from life, but the action of God in the midst of personal and human history.

Recalling the event, preserving the sources in the New Testament records, and continuing the proclamation are the vocation of the worshiping community. The purpose within Christian nurture springs from historical events and is grounded in present possibilities. It does not speak of what ought to be, or of what may be obtained by striving, but is more concerned with what is happening and can happen in the present moment. This is not to say that it excludes ultimate hopes, but only to point out that in classical Christian thought what happens ultimately is in God's hands. Yet man's situation at that ultimate point depends, to a large extent, on his present decision. Entrance into the community comes through the response to God's saving activity and is therefore concomitant with the proclamation.

Here lies the church's function as the redemptive community. Cultural education brings people the knowledge through which to use God's gifts for the greater comfort of mankind, to relieve hunger, suffering, and drudgery. Yet the further question cannot be avoided: Is "the good life" self-development or self-denial, self-fulfillment or self-giving? Realistic reading of the Bible has led some to say that the crucifixion of Jesus was not a glorious martyrdom but the ignominious end to the ever-declining popularity of a teacher who began at the crest of the wave but saw his followers fall away across the months until only a few faithful women were with him at the end. At least, that would seem to be the conclusion if modern canons of success were applied to the narrative.[14]

The insistence of cultural education that all man's powers and earth's resources be developed will form a corrective for any tendency toward a too rigid asceticism which the church might possibly set forth. But secular visions of technological progress and the successful fulfillment of democratic ideals are held in realistic focus by those who are content to live from day to day in simple witness to the way by which God accepts them as they are and liberates them into the stature of his children in Jesus Christ.

The church is the bearer of good news. This task is the call from God which makes the church a community within the cultural community for proclaiming God's activity. The fulfilling of the task yields teaching with deep implications for the lives of the members in their relationships as families, as members of the community, as citizens of a nation, and as inhabitants of the earth. This teaching can enrich the life of the member as citizen and at the same time keep him from seeing nationality in a narrow focus. Those brought up within the Christian community know from an early age that they are linked with those whom God called in ancient Israel, and in the Greco-Roman world, as well as with those who dwell within the farthest reaches of human habitation today. It is no accident that while the schools necessarily avoid facing some cultural tensions because of religious involvements, real understanding can take place between churches and synagogues as people visit with one another and share their common heritage. Tolerance is less likely to come through a discussion of ways in which people are alike than through the ability to understand the ways in which they are different and will continue to be different. Synthesis as the road to agreement is a shallow hope, for it is in the nature of human existence that each person is different from every other person.

The purposes of cultural education have been pragmatic; they have been largely concerned with activity and the results of activity. Cultural education tends to omit or at least to minimize one dimension which the Christian community insists is equally real: namely, the area of relationship to God and the recognition that life is lived in the context of eternal life. This understanding can be illustrated by the word "vocation." In common parlance, vocation refers to the fact that a person decides upon his lifework, prepares for it, and follows it. But the Latin root means a bidding, a calling, and a call must necessarily come from outside the person who is called. Therefore the Christian understands vocation as something that God does. It is his response to God's call to him; for it has been integral to Christian understanding that a person witnesses to God's saving activity within the context of everyday living. Vocation, then, would mean being guided by God in the choice, preparation, and carrying out of the work of one's life. The purposes of Christian nurture through the proclamation of the gospel involve the whole of life.

RATIONAL METHOD FOR ARRIVING AT METHODOLOGY

Cultural educators would describe their methods as "rational." Basic to their understanding is the idea of the scientific method. This appears to mean the method used by the natural sciences.

As a consequence of the principle of applying the scientific method to education, abstract reasoning holds a paramount place, because the scientific discipline requires such. Objectivity becomes a necessity. This means that a person tries to see the situation apart from himself, following the facts where they lead. Facts as objective data become the important focus for research. It is even hoped, through this method, to determine right and wrong, truth and falsehood, in a situation, so that conflicts can be resolved. Even conflicts in the sphere of ethical values can be resolved.[15]

This is the rationale of a pragmatic philosophy where experience is central and actions are judged in the light of their consequences. The "whole person" means the experiencing person as he understands himself and is intelligently comprehended by others. Respect for persons arises from the fact that personality is uniquely rational. Intelligence guides self-development and emotional control. Intelligence will convince people that they are interdependent and need to work together. William Heard Kilpatrick says, "This free play of intelligence becomes our 'sole ultimate resource' to tell us what to think and do."[16]

Theological method is also rational. It does not, however, equate rationality with the scientific method. Indeed, writers in this field make a distinction between the methodology of the natural sciences and the methodology needed for a rational interpretation of the humanities and the social sciences. In natural science the person who interprets is working with an object, an "it," but in the social sciences the interpreter is working with persons. This fact makes a difference in the kind of methods one can use. Thus each field of inquiry has the responsibility of formulating its own categories by the appropriate methods. The method of the natural sciences is descriptive; it deals with the "what" and "how." Theological method deals with the ultimate; it asks the question "why."[17] Methodology is a tool. The nature of the study determines the tool to be used.[18]

This view of the scientific method has accompanying implications. Apart from the analytical study in mathematics and the natural sciences, there is no "objectivity" in the sense that the observer can be uninvolved in the situation. The interpretation of facts gives them importance. This may be seen in the writing of history, where two researchers may begin with the same facts yet interpret them differently.[19] This happens because history is dynamic, not static; it deals with persons, not things. It refuses to yield final answers. Value judgments are there by implication.

The fact of the matter seems to be that new knowledge is based on certain premises in which one believes. Faith of some kind preceded reasoning, for presuppositions rest on faith; they are not provable in any final sense.

This method of approach is an open "system" of reasoning. One result is the frank admission of paradox. There is no attempt to resolve all conflicts and to synthesize all differences. Seeming contradiction is looked upon as a necessary ingredient of all dynamic existence, for tension is characteristic of life. Only the dead, or the inanimate, have no tension. Hence this approach is called "existential," for it is grounded in the fact of the historical, on both the personal and social levels. The individual is viewed in the wholeness of his person: physical, emotional, and intellectual. He is understood in the totality of his interrelationships, with their disharmony and conflict as well as their possibilities for creative interaction. Thus the perceptive theologian today frankly acknowledges his involvement in the life of the church whose theology he seeks to explicate.

Both cultural education and Christian education use similar rational approaches. Both understand that reasoning is essential to knowledge. Cultural education tends to be analytical to the point of verging on the impersonal. This is necessary for much of its subject matter. That approach, however, is unsuitable to the knowledge involved in Christian faith, which lies in the realm of interpersonal undertandings, grounded in history. Where God is central, his self-disclosure is also central. Where Christ is the norm, the faith relationship becomes important. When the Bible is used dynamically, there is an emphasis on the apprehension of God's activity in history. Where the context for education is the living community of the church, the existential approach gives

needed depth. The use of inductive reasoning has become axio-
matic since the time of Francis Bacon. Increasingly there is an
awareness that the thinking person is involved in what he thinks,
and a candid recognition that paradox gives the necessary multidimensional view of life which alone can prevent distortion.

Thus it is seen how two communities exist together within the
same geographical milieu. Everyone belongs to the cultural community. Some belong to the community of the church. The latter
bring into the church all the learnings that have come to them
through their life in society and this affects their interpretations
within the church. But, in addition, they have within the life of
the church a new experience. God's forgiving, renewing activity
through Christ by the Holy Spirit, which was proclaimed to them
through the life and words of other believers, sustains them
within the community of the church.

By understanding the purposes of cultural education, persons
within the church are enabled more clearly to apprehend the
unique and particular function that is given the Christian community.

There are also potential points of conflict at which the aims
of cultural educators might contradict the experience of Christians. Even if the existence of God is not openly denied, it is possible to teach in such a way as to disregard his involvement in his
world. This is implicit in asserting that the democratic ideal is the
ultimate form of corporate existence, or that men are inherently
good; that scientific method is the only respectable form of teaching; or that all problems can be solved intellectually. The faith
in inevitable progress and in the perfectibility of individuals dis-
regards what the Christian knows about sin. The unspoken assumption that life is confined to the span of earthly years needlessly limits the appreciation of the dimensions of history and
literature. " The good life " is a self-sufficient life, and the place of
defeat and self-negation is seen as a problem for man to conquer
rather than as a sacrifice man might be called upon to make for
the glory of God. Those persons who are concerned with Christian nurture need to realize these pressures, for they affect the approach to be used in communicating the faith.

The Context of Christian Education

THE COMMUNITY OF THE CHURCH

Learning takes place within a particular context. The church is the context within which Christian learning takes place. No one is a Christian in isolation. Even the anchorites of the early centuries grew up within the Christian community before they formally forsook it for a solitary existence. Knowledge of the nature of the church is needed in order to understand the kind of nurture that is offered to children and the way in which that nurture takes place.

There are many areas of knowledge about the church. There is a wide diversity in organizational patterns, in forms of worship, and in theological meanings. Yet there are some fundamental unitive understandings.[1]

Christian literature has referred to the church in the feminine gender. Although this has a grammatical basis in some languages, its significance may lie deeper than that. The church never has seemed to Christians to be an " it," a neuter " object." Existent for nearly twenty centuries, the church's very continuity provides a living quality. The church is made up of living persons under a living Lord and is empowered by the continuing presence of the Holy Spirit. This is the organic quality of the church. There are continuity, integration, and an inner wholeness which are deeper than all diversity. Perhaps this can best be explained through terms first used descriptively of the church.

Ekklēsia is one of these. Originally it meant an assembly of

36

citizens summoned by the crier. This brings to mind a picture from ancient Greece, but in the first century it was also being used to describe the synagogue. The Christian *ekklēsia* is not just any gathering of people: it is the congregation of the faithful in Jesus Christ. They met together on the first day of the week for their common worship, but they were conscious of being a part of that congregation as they went about their daily tasks.

The apostles were sure that the church was a part of the intent of Jesus. He had gathered about himself a special group, taught them, sent them out on a special mission. He knew that there were some in whom the seed of the gospel would grow and bear fruit: those who would sell all to obtain the pearl of great price. He also knew that it would be rejected of men. Yet all he left was this small community of faithful disciples.

Those who were thus called together formed an unbroken continuity across the centuries, and today the church encircles the earth. In the depth of its being the church always is aware that it did not bring itself into existence, nor can it take pride in continuity as such. It was " bought with a price " (I Cor. 6:20).

There is a further implication in the definition of *ekklēsia*. These people were not gathering from a common intention of their own: they were summoned. The first Christians knew themselves to be *electoi,* those who are called out, the elect. They did not regard themselves as a part of some great new fact of history discontinuous with all of God's past action. Rather, they felt that in them God was continuing his purpose begun in the distant past. This is not an election in the usual sense of the word, such as the acknowledgment of popularity or superiority, an opportunity for honor, power, and wealth. People would not ordinarily seek this sort of election, for it is a calling away from an accustomed pattern of living, a redirected existence. Abraham was called out of Ur and led his tribe into Canaan. Moses was called from among the Midianites and led his people through the wilderness. Saul was taken from the care of his father's flock and put at the head of his people. All these were called by God for a purpose within the community and were sustained by him accordingly. The disciples were similarly called, and what seemed to the world to be leading only to inglorious death was received by them as the glad fulfillment of life in their Lord.

Across the centuries, those persons who have responded to God's call and become partakers of this new life in Christ have strengthened one another in fellowship. This "calling" is the basis for the "gathering together" of the people of God. They are known by their *koinōnia,* the fellowship which is a distinctive mark of the Christian community. This fellowship denotes an act of mutual participation. The disciples had shared first in the earthly life of Jesus, then in the presence of the resurrected Lord. Later they were held together in the fellowship of the Holy Spirit. The fellowship is multidimensional: God seeks man, and man, through the grace of God, responds in faith. Aware of his new life he becomes a part of the community.

Basically this is not fellowship on a social level, although it may include that. Nor is it necessarily a group of "like-minded" people, for the people of this fellowship have not chosen each other but have been chosen of God. This fellowship could exist only because its members loved their Lord above all things, even life itself. They cannot be described only in terms of shared worship. They shared with those in need; indeed, among the first Christians at Jerusalem some held all possessions in common. (See Acts 4:32.) They shared persecution and they shared death. This continues today.

This fellowship is made possible by the work of the Holy Spirit in the life of the church. The Holy Spirit is the power of God active through his people in the church for making known his saving purpose among mankind. In the New Testament this is looked upon as the fact of experience through which the church grew. They had faith, they had a gathering, and in God's own time they received the gift of the Holy Spirit. Only then were they able to proclaim the gospel and to move men by their witness. The fellowship is continued by God's work through the Holy Spirit, according to the book of The Acts of the Apostles. To those outside, the church was (and is) a miscellaneous group who show a sense of purpose in time of stress, although at other times it is not always apparent what draws the people together. Yet those who are at the deep center of the church's life know that they are drawn by One who is beyond them and yet with them, and they feel in their lives a power which ministers through them in order to minister to them.

This fellowship makes possible the relatedness of persons to one another through which true nurture can take place. The growing child, sensitive to the orientation of the adults among whom he moves, is aware of this kind of fellowship when he is brought into it. It is the testimony by which he is enabled to appropriate the faith into his own life and make his own confession.

The Holy Spirit is active in the life of the church through his continuing activity in the life of the believer. One is brought to the terse words of the New Testament: " No one can say ' Jesus is Lord ' except by the Holy Spirit " (I Cor. 12:3). There were many who knew Jesus in the flesh — Pharisees and rulers, wealthy and poor, family and strangers. They speculated as to who he was: Elijah, John the Baptist, or perhaps one of the prophets; but Peter alone called him Christ. " And Jesus answered him, ' Blessed are you, Simon Bar-Jona! For flesh and blood has not revealed this to you, but my Father who is in heaven.' " (Matt. 16:17.) By the work of the Holy Spirit a person sees God in Christ and apprehends the love that seeks, suffering even to the cross, that the world through him might be saved. Yielding to that gracious call, he finds new life and becomes aware of the fellowship into which he is called.

Another work of the Holy Spirit is to empower the church in witnessing before the world. The first Christians knew about this. Out of the fires of persecution came the words: " And when they bring you to trial and deliver you up, do not be anxious beforehand what you are to say; but say whatever is given you in that hour, for it is not you who speak, but the Holy Spirit " (Mark 13:11).

The church always has been judged in the persons of those who call themselves Christian. Once they have made their confession of faith, they have placed their lives in a new context. There is a once-and-for-allness about it. If they renounce their confession, they are apostate. If they accommodate it to secular thinking, that also marks them. Life cannot ever be quite as if this act had not been made. Like it or not, they have been identified with this fellowship.

There arise times in which the church is a fellowship set apart by suffering. Then the fellowship that God imparts by his Holy Spirit is most keenly felt. It is the younger churches and the churches under persecution who are bringing a renewed sense of God made manifest in the Spirit to the attention of the church in the West. Only through this witness is the church enabled to affirm its faith. Otherwise it simply echoes the phrases of the world and is identified with the culture in which it is set. Assured of the word of the Spirit, it is enabled to proclaim the gospel according to the command of the Lord, to give the bread of life to a hungry world.

Jesus Christ is the head of the church. The organic nature of the church may be understood from the ancient view of the church as the body of which Christ is the head. The church cannot exist, much less function, without him. There can be no dichotomy between the head and the body: Christ and the church are one, for Christ indwells his church. This metaphor may be helpful to modern American thinking, where there has sometimes been a tendency to assume that the church preserves Christ rather than that he keeps the church.

The head of the body is the Lord. This is no headship in the autocratic way with which the rulers of the world view the term, although it has implied that Christ is acknowledged Lord before homage is given to Caesar. To the first Christians, in a real sense Christ was Lord over the rulers of the earth as well as over the powers of darkness and over the whole created world. An early record of apostolic preaching announces, " God has made him both Lord and Christ, this Jesus whom you crucified " (Acts 2:36).

To the church, Christ was also Lord in a deeply personal way. They gladly gave obedience to him and they confessed him before men. To him was given their complete devotion and their prayers were lifted to God in his name. They were assured that he dwelt in the midst of his people and that the life of the resurrected Lord was continued through the life of the church. This was not simply a part of their future hope of a manifestation of his Kingship. He became Lord at his resurrection and he was Lord of his church, however this might be unacknowledged or even misinterpreted by the world.

Jesus Christ was the Word made flesh. God did not send Jesus into the world to *tell* about his gracious love, but to make it known from day to day in his loving, healing, forgiving relationships with those in need, and finally in his suffering upon the cross. Through that event God became known as the God and Father of the Lord Jesus Christ.

The remembrance of Jesus and his continuing work was to be found in the community of the church. As John Knox notes, this was " not a dogmatic assertion, but a glad confession." [2] People did not accept the Lordship of Christ in order to come into the church; they came into the church because they already had become aware of his Lordship and were ready to confess it before men. The confession of Christ the Lord is one of the earliest expressions of Christian piety to be found in the New Testament. The Aramaic phrase, *Marana tha* (Our Lord, come), echoes the prayers of the first Christian groups in Galilee.

For purposes of systematic theology, the functions of the church as community, the work of the Holy Spirit, and the place of Christ are separated and categorized, but in the reality of the existential experience they are one. The church exists in order to convey the event, yet it has existence because of the event. Christ is the living presence in his church and he is made known as such by the Holy Spirit. The Spirit and the Lord are one; the Spirit testifies to Christ.

It may be seen that the church, which forms the context of the educational process, is, and always has been, a living fellowship, aware of having been brought together by the gracious action of God. The dynamic lies in the work of the Holy Spirit of God, who makes it possible for the individual to see and to respond to God's loving action, who creates fellowship, and who strengthens the church for the task of witnessing to the faith. The head is the living Christ, the Lord who is God's personal Word to mankind.

THE ORGANIC FUNCTIONING OF THE COMMUNITY

The organic functioning of the community of the church involves the production of *didachē* (teaching), this teaching being derived from the basic *kērygma* (proclamation). The living fellowship of God's people is brought together, and projected into the future, because of certain acts of God which are vital both to individuals and to the fellowship as a whole. This divine activity, put into words, is the story that the church has always proclaimed to all the world.

When dealing with the church as described here, there needs to be a careful scrutiny of what is meant by " the teaching " and how it is arrived at. This task has been made simpler by the work of recent Biblical scholars. A new dimension of Biblical understanding was opened up through the introduction of form criticism. Now, in addition to understanding the composition of the New Testament writings through an examination of their sources, there is a further aid from the delineation of the forms of literature contained therein. Oral tradition is older than the present books in the canon, and the epistles are older than the Gospels. The Christian community produced the present forms through which we know about Jesus, although the community was itself controlled by Jesus as he was known to them.

At this point the work of the British scholar C. H. Dodd becomes of primary importance. By careful interpretation of the sources, he has sought to set forth the two strands that are involved in the tradition of the primitive church: the *kērygma* and the *didachē*. His book *The Apostolic Preaching and Its Developments* [3] has had wide influence in contemporary Biblical theology.

Kērygma signifies the essential message, the proclamation. It is distinguished both from exhortation (*paraklēsis*) and the discussion of Christian living (*homilia*). The *kērygma* is the proclamation of the good news (*euangelion* — *gospel*) of the mighty acts of God whereby he has visited and redeemed his people.

The *didachē* (teaching) is derived from the *kērygma,* as we have suggested, and is also based upon it. This is the teaching section of the tradition, including the ethical content that follows from the *kērygma*. There is no assumption that those outside the church should be expected to conform to this morality. The teaching is inseparable from the proclamation in the New Testament. Whether it can ever be separated is a question, for the teaching separated from its source tends to become distorted. Without the original foundation it cannot be seen in its proper perspective. It may be that an intolerable burden is put upon people when they are exhorted to live up to an ethical ideal but are deprived of the opportunity to understand and respond to the proclamation of the good news from which that ethic originated. Before such questions are explored, it will be illuminating to outline the essentials of this all-important proclamation.

According to the Biblical accounts, groups of believers saw the risen Lord, and to such a group, according to his word, there came one day an outpouring of the Holy Spirit of God which transformed them from a waiting company into apostles filled with fire. They went forth immediately to preach the gospel in Jerusalem. The second chapter of The Acts contains the core of their proclamation, and represents probably the oldest strand of tradition as to what Jesus meant to his first followers. Here are the essential phrases:

"The age of fulfillment has dawned. . . .

"This has taken place through the ministry, death, and resurrection of Jesus. [There follows the description of his Davidic descent, ministry, death, and resurrection.] . . .

"By virtue of the resurrection, Jesus has been exalted at the right hand of God, as Messianic head of the new Israel. . . .

"The Holy Spirit in the church is the sign of Christ's present power and glory. . . .

"The Messianic Age will shortly reach its consummation in the return of Christ. . . .

"The *kērygma* always closes with an appeal for repentance, the offer of forgiveness and of the Holy Spirit, and the promise of 'salvation,' that is, of 'the life of the age to come.'" [4]

This proclamation is found also in the letters of Paul. The outline is similar to the one given in Mark 1:14-15, descriptive of the preaching of Jesus: "Jesus came into Galilee, preaching the gospel of God, and saying, 'The time is fulfilled, and the kingdom of God is at hand; repent, and believe in the gospel.'"

The Gospel of Mark is based on the *kērygma,* set in another form, with an extensive section devoted to the ministry of Jesus. The opening verse announces that purpose: "The beginning of the gospel of Jesus Christ, the Son of God." Matthew's Gospel modifies the *kērygma* by the inclusion of a large teaching section, and Luke's Gospel is a modification in its picture of the activity of Jesus. The Fourth Gospel is closest to the form developed in the Marcan Gospel. The *kērygma* is the primary material in the New Testament. It preserved the tradition which conveyed the facts basic to the Christian faith. C. H. Dodd writes:

"The nearer we are in the Gospels to the stuff of the *kērygma,* the nearer we are to the fountainhead of the tradition. There never existed a tradition formed by a dry historical interest in the facts as facts. From the beginning, the facts were preserved in memory and tradition as elements in the gospel which the church proclaimed." [5]

There is one important factor in this proclamation that is integral to any understanding of the Christian faith: it is historically oriented. It depends for its cogency and its appeal on the fact that it rests on certain well-attested historical data. It is not myth; [6] it is not a set of ideas. The Gospels were written to bear witness to God's revelation in Jesus Christ and to bring their hearers into faith. This *kērygma* is the foundation of the teaching within the fellowship of the church.

An examination of this *didachē* indicates that the ethical teaching which we find in the New Testament is not given in a body of precepts like the Jewish law, nor in a system of virtues as in Greek philosophy. Its characteristic form is "the tradition." The ethical sections of the Pauline epistles give an idea of the way in which this common ethical teaching was set before the early Christian community. Paul refers to the type of teaching to which they were committed. He opens the second chapter of First Corinthians with the words: "When I came to you, brethren, . . . I decided to know nothing among you except Jesus Christ and him crucified " (I Cor. 2:1-2) (*kērygma*). Then he adds, "Yet among the mature we do impart wisdom, although it is not a wisdom of this age or of the rulers of this age " (v. 6) (*didachē*).

Since Paul regarded the church as the body of Christ, he was confident that here would also be the sphere of divine grace. From this affirmation came a strong social ethic grounded in the teaching of Jesus. The new life that Christ brings to believers through the work of the Holy Spirit is distinguished by the ensuing action in the lives of individual believers and the Christian community. Paul writes, in Gal. 5:22-23: " The fruit of the Spirit is love, joy, peace, patience, kindness, goodness, faithfulness, gentleness, self-control; " adding, " against such there is no law." Similar ethical sections are to be found in Hebrews and First Peter.

Such teaching derives from the *kērygma* and is directly related to the Person of Jesus. Thus it is to be expected that the basic teaching material will be found in the Gospels. This part of the tradition appears primarily in the so-called Q source, a compilation of teaching material that scholars make by combining materials common to Matthew and Luke but not found in Mark. Matthew has the largest amount of the teaching materials among the Gospels. Jesus' teaching is oriented toward the absolute ethic of the Kingdom of God which now has come upon men in judgment and in mercy. " It is your Father's good pleasure to give you the kingdom." (Luke 12:32.) There is no question as to the practicality of the ethic. The grace of God which has placed men within the Kingdom gives the power to live. This is not only a guide to the good life, setting the goal and the direction; it is also the judgment of God to the conscience of men, since it shows that even the best of human attainment includes sinfulness. In so doing, it places men within the presence of God, whose mercy and forgiveness are as absolute as his demands.

The teaching material in Matthew is arranged in a fairly systematic way, as a new law given by the Messianic king. This, doubtless, is connected with the situation to which the gospel was first addressed. The deferred hope of the imminent return of the Lord was becoming adjusted to the need for a concrete way of life to guide the redeemed community within the world. Whatever in the teaching traditions of the words of Jesus suggested guidance for living came to have an especial value. This was the way in which people should live until the day of his coming.

The *kērygma* and the *didachē* may be separated for the purposes of study and definition, but note the warning of G. Ernest Wright:

> " The central message of the Bible is a proclamation of the divine action. It is impossible to reduce the *kērygma* to a kernel consisting of a series of ethical teachings. The *kērygma* is itself the kernel to which the ethics are attached and from which they receive their meaning." [7]

Here is the tradition of the Christian community: the proclamation and the teaching. It both formed and was formed by the earliest Christian groups in Jerusalem and in the Greco-Roman world of the first century. The same message has been proclaimed and taught for more than nineteen hundred years. The church today is the bearer of a teaching experience. It has no need to look afield to find something to teach. It has itself been taught. The good news has been proclaimed and the way of life taught by each generation to the succeeding one. There was no sense of newness when the first generation thus handed on the tradition. It had been so in Jewish households at the Passover time. The youngest child asked the solemn questions of the oldest man. In responsive questions and answers the recital of God's mighty acts by which he had saved Israel and brought out his chosen people was made real anew to the bearers of the heritage. (See Deut. 6:20-25.)

For the past becomes our own, not by a mere transference of words, but by the appropriation into our own life of the meaningful activity of the forebears. This is the important word: "appropriation." A catechetical recital, whether it be in the solemnity of a family Seder or the impressiveness of a ministerial visit, does not hold meaning by being an act of memorization. It can hold meaning when the words memorized take on significance for the individual as a member of the group. The Jewish child knows himself to be one of those chosen to bear witness to God's saving work through the covenant in the community of Israel. The Christian child knows himself to be one of those accepted by God for redemption through Christ within the church.

God has chosen to make himself known through events. For the Christian community, the event through which he is most fully known is his incarnation in Jesus Christ — his life, and death, and resurrection, which the *kērygma* announces. The event is historically conditioned. As such it could be simply a great memory. In reality it is more than that. The Holy Spirit represents it anew to each person within the community in each generation. The believers are enabled to appropriate the event and also by faith to become partakers in his life and death and resurrection. Thus the past becomes intelligible to a generation far removed, and they are enabled to adopt it as their own. That is why Christians can feel themselves one with the disciples who gathered around the Lord, with the martyrs who testified in the Roman Coliseum, and with the faithful who have made their witness in every century.

The past is distorted when it is made to fit into categories of the present. "Benedict and Luther must be interpreted through Christ and not vice versa. Modern human life is the scene of the activity of the Father of Jesus Christ, but Jesus can't be understood as the son of the god of modern culture." [8]

It may be seen, then, that the Christian community has at hand an accumulated and vital past which it is privileged to help the youngest generation appropriate for themselves.

THE PROCLAMATION YIELDS TEACHING

The very proclamation of the good news is teaching. It is this: "The new age has dawned. Jesus, who was sent by God, has brought it through his living and dying and his resurrection. He is the living Lord, as you can see by his Holy Spirit, who is re-creating lives through his power in the church. Turn around; accept the forgiveness that God is offering; receive the Holy Spirit; and become partakers of eternal life now and evermore." This is not "teaching" in the sense of the imparting of information. It is the dynamic word through which a redemptive experience is mediated. The way in which it is proclaimed as well as the fact of its proclamation gives a ground for interpreting the experience. When the words are appropriated by the person and he is turned around — accepting the forgiveness of God, finding new life in Jesus Christ — then he has the ground for interpreting the experience.

The *kērygma* yields teaching beyond the immediate setting forth of the story of God's activity, for it must be understood in several ways by the church itself as it seeks to establish its life in the world. The earliest way in which the church explained the *kērygma* to itself was through the sacraments. The first of these was Baptism. Although this rite was related to the baptism of John, signifying repentance and the forgiveness of sin, the early Christians understood this redemption to have been made manifest truly in the death and resurrection of Jesus Christ. The going down into the water was a re-presentation, by which the believer went down into death with the Lord; and as Jesus was raised from the dead, so the believer was baptized into eternal life through Christ and with him. "You must be born anew," says the Fourth Gospel. "Unless one is born of water and the Spirit, he cannot enter the kingdom of God." (John 3:7, 5.)

The Lord's Supper is the supreme re-presentation of the *kērygma.*[9] This is sometimes called the Eucharist, meaning a thanksgiving. It is an act of worship in which the believers participate, addressing God and praising him for his love, made known through his saving acts in the life, death, and resurrection of Jesus Christ. Through this activity the worshiping community relives the historical situation now two thousand years removed, and makes it contemporaneous by the re-presentation and personal appropriation through which, again, his body is broken and his blood shed for them. The living Lord is in the midst of his people.

The *kērygma* is further understood through the confessions. It is significant that while in English " I believe " seems to connote a passive acceptance and primarily an intellectual activity, the Greek word *pisteō* — " I faith," if it could be so translated — has an active meaning. Martin Luther has put this vividly:

> " Observe that there are two ways of believing. In the first place, I may have a faith concerning God. This is the case when I hold to be true what is said concerning God. Such faith is on the same level as the assent I give to the statements concerning the Turk, the devil, and hell. A faith of this kind should rather be called knowledge or information than faith.
>
> " In the second place, there is faith in God. Such is mine when I not only hold to be true what is said concerning God, but when I put my trust in him in such a way as to enter into personal relations with him, believing firmly that I shall find him to be and to do as I have been taught. Not in the Turk do I believe thus, nor in any other man, however highly he may be praised. . . . Such faith, which ventures everything upon what it has heard concerning God, be it life or death, constitutes the Christian man, and it receives everything of God it desires. . . . The word ' in ' is well chosen and deserving of due attention. We do not say, ' I believe God the Father,' but ' in God the Father.' . . . Such faith no one may claim but God alone." [10]

This was the situation of the first Christians. When they said, " Our Lord, come," they were expressing a faith that was the basis for their daily life; namely, that Jesus was their Lord who soon would return to make known his glorious work of salvation to all the world.

There are a number of such confessions, or creeds, in the New Testament, and it has been the work of the form-critics to uncover these through their rhythm and the thought content.[11] One of the earliest confessions preserved is quoted by Paul in Phil. 2:5-11:

> " . . . Christ Jesus,
> who though he was in the form of God,
> did not count equality with God a thing to be grasped,
> but emptied himself, taking the form of a servant,
> being born in the likeness of men.
> And being found in human form he humbled himself
>   and became obedient unto death,
>   even death on a cross.
> Therefore God has highly exalted him
>   and bestowed on him the name which is above every name,
> that at the name of Jesus every knee should bow,
>   in heaven and on earth, and under the earth,
> and every tongue confess that Jesus Christ is Lord,
>   to the glory of God the Father."

There are two points which need to be kept in mind in considering the place of the confessions in the early church. To begin with, a confession expressed the faith of the church as a group. In affirming it, one was a part of the worshiping congregation, and even if one affirmed it alone in Caesar's court, it was because of, and as a part of, the Christian fellowship. There was never a question of isolating particular statements for purposes of personal intellectual veracity. The confession itself was a whole; the meaning could only be seen in its wholeness. Again, one did not accept the confession verbally or intellectually in order to become a part of the community of the church. One wished to become a part of the fellowship because he had already responded to the gospel and already affirmed in his heart and mind that Jesus was the Lord. It was not a matter of accepting a proposition in order to become a member of the church. To affirm the confession was a privilege — and a dangerous one at that.

The *kērygma* is also understood by the church as doctrine. This is a necessary intellectual development beyond the simple confession of faith. It is an attempt to comprehend more deeply that which is only hinted at in the words of the Biblical confessions. The Scriptures of the Old Testament and the New Testament were normative as the bases for all later development of Christian thought among the church fathers.

The members of the primitive church were conscious that they knew God beyond any apprehension that had been theirs in their Judaic faith. Christ had opened to them a new and living way to the Father, and the Holy Spirit was the bearer of the knowledge of God through Christ. The word "Trinity" is not used in the New Testament, but the awareness is there. Consider this sentence, cited above, from Philippians: "And being found in human form he humbled himself and became obedient unto death, even death on a cross." (Phil. 2:8.) This does not describe, in any ordered way, the saving work of Christ, but it raises questions that require deeper probing under the guidance of the Holy Spirit, until across the centuries an Irenaeus and an Anselm wrote their affirmations to the glory of God and for the understanding of their fellow Christians. The "babes in Christ" whom Paul addressed at Corinth expected an early return of their Lord, but the Christian hope is still a subject for study by Christians witnessing amidst a hostile world.

Theology is derived from such dedicated searching. G. Ernest Wright has a pointed statement on the subject:

> "Biblical theology is not propositional dogmatics, stated abstractly and universally in accordance with a coherent system. It is a theology of recital or proclamation of the acts of God, together with the inferences drawn therefrom." [12]

Christian doctrine should not be developed as an abstract system of thought, but must always remain true to the historical context of events from which it sprang. This is the safeguard by which it is kept from being "propositional" and enabled to be "existential." Whenever the cross itself is seen as central — and not any abstract ideas *about* the cross — theology will be dynamic.

The *ķērygma* yields further teaching as the church seeks to understand its moral implications. One does not find abstract ideals here, either; nor a set of principles by which life must be lived on some Kantian plane of duty. The teaching needs to be seen more broadly as the theory of the Christian life. Herein lies its significance for day-to-day existence. The good news transforms all of life. Those who have received God's graciousness in forgiveness and newness of life are "new creatures in Christ." The words they speak in joy are authenticated in lives of loving service. Augustine, writing his commentary on the Sermon on the Mount, speaks of the Beatitudes as giving a picture of the redeemed life. In his exegesis of "Blessed are the peacemakers," for instance, he deals primarily with a quality of life in which the person is responsive to God. Thus one becomes peaceful within oneself, not in order to give an example so that others will become peaceful, but in order that one may show forth this quality of life to the world.[13]

There is need to guard against seeing the Sermon on the Mount only as a new law. The requirements of the Christian life are set over against and beyond that demanded in the law:

> "You have heard that it was said to the men of old, 'You shall not kill; and whoever kills shall be liable to judgment.' But I say to you that every one who is angry with his brother shall be liable to judgment; whoever insults his brother shall be liable to the council, and whoever says, 'You fool!' shall be liable to the hell of fire." (Matt. 5:21-22.)

A human being could hardly achieve that standard by repression, sublimation, or any other standard of his own. Rather, "the fruit of the Spirit is peace, . . . gentleness." The answer lies there. This does not tell people how they *must* live but how they *shall* live when they are indwelt by the Holy Spirit. The teaching finds in the vital *ķērygma* the dynamic for the Christian life, experienced in specific situations.

On the surface it would seem that Luke's picture of Jesus fits the didactic purpose, for here seems to be a figure who is an inviting "example." It would not appear to have been thus to those first Christians. They knew that he had brought them salvation. They could live for him; they could die for him; they could obey and follow him; but they knew that they could never, by any imitation, become the incarnate Word of God. Thus, when the Christian reads the Gospels, he does not identify with Jesus, but with those who sought Jesus. He is the father crying, "I believe; help my unbelief!" (Mark 9:24). He is the centurion saying, "Lord, do not trouble yourself, for I am not worthy to have you come under my roof" (Luke 7:6). He is Peter saying, "You are the Christ" (Mark 8:29).

Yet the teachings of Jesus cannot be abstracted from his life. The epistles contain many allusions to the life of the Lord as the foundation on which the ethic is placed. "Be kind to one another, tenderhearted, forgiving one another, as God in Christ forgave you." (Eph. 4:32.) All teaching goes back to this historic point of reference. "Be kind to one another," as church schools have so often taught their kindergarten children to repeat, is not a simple humanitarian principle. It is rooted in the love of God made known through his action in Jesus. Nor are people bidden simply to "love one another" — as though that were easy for children or for adults. The writer of the Johannine literature affirms: "Beloved, let us love one another; for love is of God, and he who loves is born of God and knows God. He who does not love does not know God; for God is love." (I John 4:7-8.) Again, in the same writing, "We love, because he first loved us" (I John 4:19).

The Christian is not an observer giving rules from the book to be followed. He is a participant, and his whole life is bound up in the response that he makes to what he reads in the gospel. Paul said that for him the function of the law was to show him how unable he was to fulfill its demands by his own striving. (See Rom. 7:7 ff.) The teaching may serve to bring the Christian into an ever-deepening relationship to God who saves him, while for those who live joyously in the grace of God it is the picture of the redeemed life.

The teaching has another function. The Christian always has been aware that there is a sense in which he is in the world but not of the world. He has been the recipient of the saving love of the holy and gracious God. He is part of a community that bears witness to this fact and proclaims it as an invitation to the whole world. He looks at life from a different angle. Having asked and received the answer to the primary question, " What must I do to be saved? " he now asks the question, " How do we live who are saved? " It is written: " If you salute only your brethren, what more are you doing than others? Do not even the Gentiles do the same? " (Matt. 5:47.) One thing is clear from the New Testament records: being a Christian meant being " different," being set apart. It was a vocation, a call from God. It was not, at first, a puritanical separateness. The new Christian avoided his pagan environment as much as possible in order that he might not be led into temptation. Those who were mature in the faith did not need the same kind of experiences. They were witnesses *in* the world to eternal life which was their present joy. It was a " different " kind of existence.

Thus varied, the *kērygma* yields teaching for the fellowship within the church. It interprets the redemptive experience which it mediates; it is understood through sacraments, confessions, and doctrine; it provides the basis for the Christian life of the individual.

The nature of the *kērygma* requires that it be shared with all others. This inward compulsion to proclaim the gospel produces the evangelistic task. The church must ask itself how to express the good news in terms of the situation that the people of any generation face.[14] This is essentially what every missionary does as he goes into a country whose people are unfamiliar with the Christian faith. This is how John Wesley preached to the English crowds in the eighteenth century, arresting their attention as they were on their way to work in the early morning. This is what T. S. Eliot is trying to do in some of his poetry, addressed to the sophisticated aesthetes or intellectuals of this day.

The propagation of the faith depends on such proclamation, and the continuation of the visible fellowship requires it. Since the *kērygma* is not a set of abstract propositions but is the record of God's saving activity in history, it must be spoken in such a way that the event is remembered and made contemporary. This is not an easy task and can be done only by those who have appropriated the gospel into their very lives. The objective observer cannot help, for although he may be interested intellectually or aesthetically, he is not committed.

The *kērygma* yields further teaching as the community of the church faces the necessity to explain its life to the world — the apologetic task. Justin Martyr (died ca. 165) was one of the first apologists within the church. Christians were beginning to be noticed in the Empire, and sporadic early persecutions had not had any effect toward eradicating this new sect. Writers were beginning to cast accusations meant to undermine the relationships between Christians and their fellow citizens. Justin Martyr tried to reply to this by setting forth an explanation of the faith in terms that he hoped would be understandable to his readers. This was not easy to do, for the Biblical modes of thought, so characteristic of first-century Christianity, were not always translatable into Greek terms. From that day onward, apologetics has meant trying to express a Biblical faith in philosophical forms. Some have thought that this is impossible. Others, aware of the dangers of distortion, still have felt it necessary to make the attempt. Paul Tillich's theologizing in terms of existential philosophy is an example of the latter effort, while Karl Barth has forsaken all such attempts in the later volumes of his theology.

In every century there are people living within the immediate environment of the church who know nothing about it or who deliberately turn from it. These feel that the church is useless and even harmful: impeding progress, using wrong methods of dealing with people; holding an out-of-date cosmogony, anthropology, or historical framework. The numerous objections do not seem to vary, save in phraseology, from generation to generation. To these objectors the church addresses its apologetic, seeking to explain its understandings in such a way as to correct false impressions and win for itself a degree of toleration by which to do the tasks of education and evangelization. The apologetic task is not the same as the proclamatory, and these should not be confused. Apologetics will hardly win the commitment of the whole self to a new way of life, for it is not primarily addressed to the whole self. It is an appeal to the heart and mind of those who are against the church that they may understand it and permit it to continue its task. This is a necessity today for the church: in Asia, beset by nationalism, and in Europe and America, surrounded by secularism. When the church fails to see the need for the apologetic task, it may be that it has so far conformed itself to the prevailing culture that neither its own people nor those outside see anything difficult or dangerous within the gospel.

TEACHING FROM THE FELLOWSHIP

While the teaching in the church is derived mainly from the proclamation, the fellowship (*koinōnia*) also yields teaching, similarly based on the proclamation. This arises first of all out of the need for mutual strengthening. The church is always in danger. There may be the threat of physical extinction, such as was faced during the Diocletian persecution which began in A.D. 303, in the Communist antagonism against Christianity in Russia, especially during the 1920's, or in the recurring harassments in China. Threat of absorption is seen by sensitive Christians, who are concerned lest the gospel be equated with any particular social order in such measure that its distinctive nature be eclipsed. Whenever an external situation produces threat or concern, the members of the fellowship draw nearer to one another. In worship, testimony, and activity they recall God's gracious action toward them in Jesus Christ. They explain to themselves why this present situation has arisen. They strengthen one another with assurance so that they will be mutually enabled to make a good confession before the world. The writing of the New Testament book The Revelation to John appears to have been motivated in part by the desire to provide such mutual encouragement within the fellowship in a time of persecution.

The fellowship yields further teaching in the task of explaining to one another the meaning of the redemptive experience.

This particular type of explaining springs from a subjective understanding which seeks to comprehend the significance of the experience for the totality of faith. It may even be expressed symbolically rather than verbally. This was especially true of much of the symbolism of the primitive church. The simple outline of the fish would communicate nothing to the observer, but to the believer it signified Jesus Christ, the Son of God, the Savior. The cross had a far different interpretation within the Christian community from that which it had for the rest of the world. The epistles illustrate another way in which this explaining took place. When Paul and others wrote to the young Christian communities, their letters were reread, treasured, and copied as they were sent from place to place for mutual sharing. Hymnody is another form of such explaining. Whereas the Gregorian modes expressed the objective worship of the congregation, such affirmations as " A Mighty Fortress Is Our God " and other hymns of Martin Luther's, as well as the Genevan psalm settings and the hymns of the Wesleys, are eloquent testimony to this kind of explaining. Consider Charles Wesley's words:

> " O for a thousand tongues to sing
> My great Redeemer's praise,
> The glories of my God and King,
> The triumphs of his grace."

Poetry and drama are further expressions of the same phenomenon. These are not merely methods of communication; they produce a particular type of explanation which is in itself an addition to the interpretative teaching of the church.

This ability to explain is a gift of the Holy Spirit. Paul speaks of it in his letter to the Corinthians, when he refers to the variety of spiritual gifts.

> " To each is given the manifestation of the Spirit for the common good. To one is given through the Spirit the utterance of wisdom, and to another the utterance of knowledge according to the same Spirit, to another faith by the same Spirit, to another gifts of healing by the one Spirit, to another the working

of miracles, to another prophecy, to another the ability to distinguish between spirits, to another various kinds of tongues, to another the interpretation of tongues." (I Cor. 12:7-10.)

The gifts may be different in the modern church, but the fellowship is still strengthened as Christians indulge in this mutual explaining.

The fellowship always has yielded teaching also as a nurturing of those who are new and those who are young in the faith. The catechetical instruction of the early church is an example. The catechumens were assembled for a period of learning during which the meaning of the Creed and the sacraments was explained to them. When the culture became predominantly Christian and consequently there were fewer adult converts, this catechetical instruction was given to baptized children to prepare them for confirming their baptismal vows and for receiving the Lord's Supper. Instruction was added in the meaning of the Lord's Prayer and the Ten Commandments. Such instruction was continued in various forms and is still offered in some churches. The Westminster Catechism, which has become a classic of Christian instruction, consists of a series of questions and answers concisely outlining the great affirmations of the faith. It is reminiscent of the Old Testament incidents in which God addresses his chosen one, and the person thus addressed makes reply. Or one thinks of the threefold questioning of Peter by the risen Lord in the Johannine narrative. Thus, in the catechism, when the minister of Christ addresses the child, already baptized in the faith, the child responds by indicating that he is a participant in the tradition and that he is in process of appropriating it to himself.

" Q. How are we made partakers of the redemption purchased by Christ?

" A. We are made partakers of the redemption purchased by Christ by the effectual application of it to us by his Holy Spirit.

" Q. How doth the Spirit apply to us the redemption purchased by Christ?

" A. The Spirit applieth to us the redemption purchased by Christ by working faith in us, and thereby uniting us to Christ in our effectual calling." [15]

How catechetical instruction is to be carried on is quite another question, and present-day usages are receiving serious consideration, particularly among Roman Catholic and Lutheran educators. The curriculum of the modern church school is a way by which the community of the church tries to present the *kērygma* to children so that it may become meaningful in terms of their needs as they grow within the fellowship.

Finally, the fellowship yields teaching as a channel through which to make the gospel relevant to the ever-changing situations in which the church's people must live. Again, the epistles come to mind. One can almost reconstruct the questions which had been sent to Paul as one reads his answers. Dare a Christian eat meat offered to idols? How are quarrels to be settled? These, and how many more!

The homily grew out of this same concern of the fellowship. It was a simple talk given during the service to point out how the Christian ought to live. This seems to have been the predominating type of preaching during the Middle Ages. It drew on the Bible for illustrations rather than beginning with the Biblical text and exploring the implications for living. Martin Luther's preaching was usually more Biblical. Preaching in the first half of the twentieth century tended to be a setting forth of the teaching in terms of daily living.

It may be seen, then, that the church, which is the context for Christian nurture, is the bearer of a redemptive activity which the members have experienced within it. This activity is the *kērygma*, which both forms the church and is formed by it. The *kērygma* yields teaching, expressed in the words of the confessions and the activity of the sacraments, intellectualized in doctrine, and made relevant to the immediate situation in terms of ethics. The *kērygma* further yields teaching through the fellowship — explaining the redemptive experience, nurturing children, and strengthening the community for witnessing in the world.

The Content of Christian Education

THE ACTIVITY OF GOD

From its start, the church always had a specific word to speak about God. It could not have been only the word that had been spoken in the covenant, the Law and the Prophets, or the men of Jerusalem would hardly have listened. It could not have been only the lofty spiritual precepts of the philosophers, else the people of Ephesus and Philippi and Rome would not have listened. A careful examination of the proclamation indicates something of how it spoke to men about God.

To begin with, he is the living God and he is known through his activity. "Jesus of Nazareth, a man attested to you by God with mighty works and wonders and signs which God did through him in your midst, as you yourselves know." (Acts 2:22.) Jesus is announced in the *kērygma* in terms of that which God has done. God has taken the initiative and has made himself known in the man Jesus Christ. Man does not need to seek God, for God has already been seeking man. "For the promise is to you and to your children and to all that are far off, every one whom the Lord our God calls to him." (Acts 2:39.) This affirmation that God is his own discloser is as old as the Bible and as new as the latest books affirming God in a scientific age. Karl Heim writes:

> "God is not an It, since no I could be generated from an It. And so God can never, as is always possible in the case of an It, be the object of my action, to examine it microscopically or to

record it photographically. So long as I endeavor, as a cool, scientific observer, to discover God from the effects which he produces, I see nothing of God. There can be no meeting with him. Nor can I find God by immersing myself in myself. . . . I can find God only if he meets me as my Thou." [1]

If God is known only through his own activity, it becomes important to understand the nature of such activity. The Bible witnesses to his saving work among men. In Peter's proclamation of the gospel on the day of Pentecost, he quotes from the prophet Joel and from the Psalms to indicate this work of God: "Thou hast made known to me the ways of life; thou wilt make me full of gladness with thy presence" (Acts 2:28). There is a modern equivalent in the words of the General Thanksgiving spoken by the congregation in the office of Morning Prayer of *The Book of Common Prayer:* "We bless thee for our creation, preservation, and all the blessings of this life; but above all, for thine inestimable love in the redemption of the world by our Lord Jesus Christ."

This was indeed good news. God is not an idea; he is not a power to be feared. God is the living God, who actively wills to save mankind, and who has shown his saving purpose through his incarnation. Here one comes to the heart of the gospel: namely, that He who is personal has most fully made himself known through a Person. "In many and various ways God spoke of old to our fathers by the prophets; but in these last days he has spoken to us by a Son." (Heb. 1:1-2.) It has always been a profound mystery in Christian faith that the eternal God should so humble himself as to share the limitations of earthly life, yet many have so believed. Paul writes to the Colossians, "For in him all the fullness of God was pleased to dwell" (Col. 1:19).

God has made himself known in a Person who lived, who had friends and foes, who suffered and died. The church reaffirms this whenever the Creed is spoken: "suffered under Pontius Pilate." Christianity is a historical religion and what it has to say about God is set in a historic framework. When the Gospels set forth the story of Jesus, they are showing the character of God.

When the proud are rebuked, the sorrowing comforted, the sick healed, or sinners forgiven, the Gospels are saying, "God is like this."

From this activity of God in Christ, the first Christians were able to see the work of creation in a new light. If God had gone to such lengths to awaken men's love, surely he had always loved men. The echoes of the first chapter of Genesis are too clear to go unrecognized in the reading of the opening of the Fourth Gospel:

> "In the beginning was the Word, and the Word was with God, and the Word was God. He was in the beginning with God; all things were made through him, and without him was not anything made that was made." (John 1:1-3.)

Or in the words of Paul to the church at Corinth: "For it is the God who said, 'Let light shine out of darkness,' who has shone in our hearts to give the light of the knowledge of the glory of God in the face of Christ" (II Cor. 4:6).

There were some people, then as now, who were not sure that God was the Lord of all creation. They feared that demonic powers threatened his sway, or that part of the world was under the power of evil. To such the gospel spoke with joyous power. God who has shown his love in Jesus Christ is indeed the ruler of all the world. This is said in the hymn from The Revelation to John (ch. 4:11):

> "Worthy art thou, our Lord and God,
> to receive glory and honor and power,
> for thou didst create all things,
> and by thy will they existed and were created."

Glad as the New Testament writers were to show that the creative activity of God indicated his Lordship over all nature, they found their deepest assurance of faith in the fact that creation made known God's love and concern for the creatures whom he had made. Paul wrote, "If any one is in Christ, he is a new creation." (II Cor. 5:17.) From the beginning of the world, God made man for communion with himself. Christian faith affirms that the nature of God is love. Love is most fully satisfied when there is another to whom love can be given and from whom love may be received. God is self-sufficient. He did not need to make man, or create a world in which man could dwell. Although God's work continues, he is not merely to be identified with the creative process. He creates and sustains by whatever process he chooses to employ.

This Christian understanding of God's activity as the Creator is properly to be seen as a religious understanding. The psalmist prays, "Create in me a clean heart, O God." (Ps. 51:10.) God's creative activity in the beginning is continued through the events of history and in the ever-present work of his Holy Spirit in the lives of his people through the church. The writer of Ephesians says:

> "For he has made known to us in all wisdom and insight the mystery of his will, according to his purpose which he set forth in Christ as a plan for the fullness of time, to unite all things in him, things in heaven and things on earth." (Eph. 1:9-10.)

"The fullness of time" is a phrase that denotes the linkage between God's work in creation and his work in history. God created time. "In the beginning God created the heavens and the earth. . . . And there was evening and there was morning, one day." (Gen. 1:1, 5.) Thereafter God made himself known through events. In particular, for reasons unknown to mortal men, he chose a small group of people living in an unpromising little country and through the centuries he prepared them for his revelation in Jesus Christ.

God is the Lord of history. Some of the oldest historical records in existence are to be found in the Old Testament. Those were written, as their phraseology indicates, not to extol the mighty acts of kings, but to bear witness to the saving activity of Yahweh toward his chosen people. That God should govern the destiny of a people is as much a cause of wonder as that he, himself the uncreated, should have created a world, yet the two are linked. Herbert Butterfield, who is primarily a historian rather than a theologian, yet writes: "The God of history certainly turns out to be the God of nature too; and once we have laid hold of the conception of man-in-history we can then safely go forward to discover how deeply man himself is rooted in earthiness." [2] From this it may be seen that although the Bible is uniquely "holy history," God's activity in history may not be confined to the events therein narrated, but he is now, as then, the Lord of history, for history too is a part of creation.

This view has been referred to by the term "providence," indicating God's desire to save and to re-create. The understanding of God's providential activity gives a sense of security to his creatures who see therein an evidence of his love. It should not be interpreted mechanically in such a way that man becomes a puppet rather than a free being, as the Christian believes God intended him to be. Love can be given only freely and by personal decision. God created man in order that man might love his Creator. His providential care is a part of God's self-disclosure, seeking man's response in faith and trust.

The creation of the world and of time and God's providential guidance in history are linked with the ultimate purposes of his sustaining care — the goal toward which history moves. This is seen throughout the Old Testament, especially in the work of the prophets. God had chosen Israel for a purpose; God would visit and redeem his people in his own time.

To understand this ultimate purpose as it appeared to the writers of the New Testament, it is necessary to divest oneself of nineteenth-century ideas of inevitable progress. The ominous words, "When the Son of man comes, will he find faith on earth?" (Luke 18:8) indicate uncertainty as to the possibilities of the future. The vivid pictures of woe in The Revelation to John indicate a belief that the times lying immediately ahead will be fearful. Yet faith in God as the Creator, Lord, and Redeemer of his people gave assurance that the ultimate victory would be his.

The first words that the writer of Mark's Gospel puts on the lips of Jesus are, "The time is fulfilled, and the kingdom of God is at hand; repent, and believe in the gospel " (Mark 1:14). God's ultimate purpose, his reign over his people, is begun with the coming of his Son Jesus Christ. Complete fulfillment awaits his return to reveal his glory at the end of history, but the new age has already broken into history.[3] As the years merged into centuries, and the centuries into millenniums, the disciples of the Lord learned to understand the patience implied in the words, " Watch therefore, for you know neither the day nor the hour " (Matt. 25:13). In every dismaying circumstance, the church has always held the assurance that God would ultimately reveal Jesus as the Lord before all mankind, and not only to the faithful ones who responded to his call.

While this is not the only answer given concerning the evil in the world, it indicates the Christian affirmation that evil must be seen in relationship to a loving God whose creative and sustaining power made the world, keeps the world, and has a purpose in human history.

Human beings have found various ways of enduring bravely the buffets of life. Some have sublimated their sufferings in their activities for others; some have repressed their sufferings and sought to seem indifferent. The witness of the Christian faith has been that God has transformed evil, making it serve his redemptive purpose. The omnipotence of God comes to mean not merely an unlimited power to do as he pleases, but the loving power by which man can be permitted freedom while the evil that man might purpose can be turned to serve the glory of God.

The question of justice is not man's but God's. Paul wrote:

> " For there is no distinction; since all have sinned and fall short of the glory of God, they are justified by his grace as a gift, through the redemption which is in Christ Jesus." (Rom. 3:22-24.)

This is what some contemporary theologians refer to as a " paradox " of the Christian faith. How can that event which was made to show God's love also reveal his judgment or his wrath? This happens because any event can only be understood in terms of its meanings to the individuals who are confronted by it. The writer of the Fourth Gospel foreshadows the final rejection of Jesus by an earlier incident:

> "After this many of his disciples drew back and no longer went about with him. Jesus said to the twelve, 'Will you also go away?' Simon Peter answered him, 'Lord, to whom shall we go? You have the words of eternal life; and we have believed, and have come to know, that you are the Holy One of God.'" (John 6:66-69.)

Contrary to some popular opinion in the modern world, the crucifixion was not by itself redemptive. There were many, in that day, who witnessed the agony of the Son of God on Calvary. One thief reviled him; another sought forgiveness. Some mocked him; a centurion recognized him. The passing crowd saw a criminal hanged; the faithful saw the hope of Israel slain.

The saving love of God was shown in the resurrection, and that was revealed only to the faithful. Jesus became for them "the first fruits of those who have fallen asleep" (I Cor. 15:20). No matter what evil or suffering men might hereafter endure through one another's sins, this much was certain: God understood. For he had experienced the cruelty, the evil, and the suffering of the cross; and God would give the victory even as he already had done through Jesus Christ the Lord.

The Christian church has always affirmed that in Christ God has made the whole creation new. Paul wrote: "For the creation waits with eager longing for the revealing of the sons of God; . . . because the creation itself will be set free from its bondage to decay and obtain the glorious liberty of the children of God." (Rom. 8:19, 21.) Then, encompassing all the powers of the world that have struggled against the purposes of God, he cries out exultantly:

> "For I am sure that neither death, nor life, nor angels, nor principalities, nor things present, nor things to come, nor powers, nor height, nor depth, nor anything else in all creation, will be able to separate us from the love of God in Christ Jesus our Lord." (Rom. 8:38-39.)

THE SAVING WORK OF GOD

The gospel is known through the community of the church. In the New Testament the gospel is identified with certain phrases through which it is proclaimed to all hearers. The " good news " is not stated abstractly, but always is expressed within a particular situation. The first chapters of The Acts of the Apostles record the apostle Peter's announcement of this good news. When Peter testified to what God had done through Christ, he was brought before the court. When he appeared before the elders, he did not plead his case, but merely repeated his testimony. This was the man who had left his fisherman's boat on the Lake of Galilee to follow Jesus, and who at Caesarea Philippi had acknowledged him to be the Christ. He had shared the glory of the Mount of Transfiguration and the agony of the Garden of Gethsemane. This man had denied his Master during the trial and was one of the first to receive the message that the Lord was risen. None of the accounts so movingly expresses Peter's own deep need for reconciliation as does the Fourth Gospel when it depicts Jesus' asking him, " Do you love me? " and gives Peter's reply: " Yes, Lord; you know that I love you " (John 21:15-19).

The good news is first given to the people of Jerusalem from the lips of Peter. Seemingly the words are meant to be understood in conjunction with him who speaks them. They could not have been said by just anyone. They would not have been said in the same tone of voice by the high priest who was antagonistic, or a Roman soldier who might be scornful, or a traveler within the city who could be indifferent. It had to be one like Peter, with all his background of confession, betrayal, and reconciliation, who spoke the message. It said, in effect, " You see me; you know who I am; now understand by these words what has happened to me."

What had happened to Peter, as the first chapter of The Acts of the Apostles indicates, was that the Holy Spirit had come upon him. When the apostles spoke by the Spirit, their listeners faced a time of decision. They might respond as on the Day of

Pentecost: "Now when they heard this they were cut to the heart, and said to Peter and the rest of the apostles, 'Brethren, what shall we do?'" (Acts 2:37). But they might also react as they did to the rebuke of Stephen: "Now when they heard these things they were enraged, and they ground their teeth against him. . . . Then they cast him out of the city and stoned him" (Acts 7:54, 58).

The gospel is truly heard when it is spoken by one who has received it into his life. It is not a concept to be intellectually apprehended, nor a statement of belief to be accepted, but a reality understood through participation. The gospel is an act of God which results in a new way of living. When the Philippian jailer saw that his prisoners had not made their escape although the prison doors were open, he said, "Men, what must I do to be saved?" (Acts 16:30). Paul and Silas replied, "Believe in the Lord Jesus, and you will be saved, you and your household." (V. 31.) The man recognized that he must *do* something, and Paul's reply, to believe in the Lord Jesus, must have meant a radical change in life pattern.

The writers of the Gospel narratives depict this same necessity for involvement. There is the story of the call of Levi, to whom Jesus said, "Follow me," and he rose up and followed him. (See Matt. 9:9-13; Mark 2:13-17; Luke 5:27-32.) The rich young ruler came to Jesus asking what he must do to have eternal life. When Jesus said, "Go, sell what you possess and give to the poor, . . . and come, follow me," his countenance fell at the saying, and "he went away sorrowful." (See Matt. 19:16-30; Mark 10:17-31; Luke 18:18-30.) Only by receiving the good news into one's life could it be truly understood.

This gospel not only proclaims God's work, but shows forth his activity. Since the person speaking is always one who has responded to God, what he has to say is never theoretical. He is not enumerating the possible ways in which God might act, but witnessing to the way he has known God to act. When Paul spoke before King Agrippa, he began by giving the story of his own life, recounting both his persecution of the followers of Jesus (at the time when he knew *about* Jesus but had not responded to him) and his encounter on the Damascus road. He says, " I was not disobedient to the heavenly vision, but declared first to those at Damascus, then at Jerusalem and throughout all the country of Judea, and also to the Gentiles, that they should repent and turn to God and perform deeds worthy of their repentance." He concludes with the proclamation of the gospel. (See Acts 26:1-23.)

God's action takes place in and through the fellowship. It is seen through human relationships within the church before it confronts the observer outside the church. People come into the church because they have known God's love toward them, proclaimed and made manifest through the Christian community.

Through the *kērygma* the hearer is offered the forgiveness of sins. "Repent therefore, and turn again, that your sins may be blotted out." (Acts 3:19.)

The forgiveness of sins would be of concern to a person who was trying hard to live a good life, according to whatever standards of goodness he had set before himself. To the Jew this meant the law, which was God's precious gift to his people. It is written, " But his delight is in the law of the Lord, and on his law he meditates day and night " (Ps. 1:2). Paul was such a man in his early days. Such a person would be worried because of his lapses, his seeming inability to live up to the law. In modern parlance this might be understood as "falling short of one's ideals." He stood self-condemned.

Forgiveness of sins would also be of concern to the person who had fallen utterly into the depths, but who somehow saw a ray of hope. Such was the condition of the paralytic, so helpless that four friends had to carry him to Jesus (Mark 2:3-5). This was the siutation of the woman taken in adultery (John 8:2-11). Such was the need of large numbers of people in that day who, because of the long hours of work required for earning a living, had not enough time to fulfill the ritual exactions that would make them good sons of the law.

The theological term for forgiveness is "justification." It means " to make just." God is holy, and no one may stand before his presence in sin. The covenant was the promise of God's presence among his people — the assurance that even if they sinned and were punished they would always be restored. The law showed them what the covenant required. One could always know exactly where he stood in relation to God. But to the conscientious, and to the lost, the law could only bring despair. God himself must deliver his people; only he could "make just."

The new word which these Christians spoke was that God had made known his forgiveness through Jesus. The community that knew him as the Lord understood the meaning of his life and work. God had come to meet man: "The Word became flesh and dwelt among us" (John 1:14).

Jesus is the Savior. Modern man asks why God chose this way of releasing men from sin and giving them new life. The question is an old one; it is the title of Anselm's book, written in the twelfth century: *Cur Deus Homo?* (Why Did God Become Man?).[4] The Bible affirms that God is the seeking God. This is seen in the parable of the forgiving father (Luke 15:11-32) and in the parable of the lost sheep (Luke 15:3-7). It is poignantly set forth in the parable of the man who planted a vineyard, then let it out to tenants and went into another country. He sent messengers and finally a beloved son. "And they took him and killed him." (See Mark 12:1-11.)

By entering directly into human life, God could know man through participation in his existence. Jesus was "one who in every respect has been tempted as we are, yet without sinning" (Heb. 4:15).

By showing how much he cared, God could draw men toward him. The first chapter of Mark's Gospel relates how Jesus is baptized, is tempted, preaches "the gospel of God," calls four disciples, teaches in the synagogue, casts out a demon, heals a woman's fever, heals many people, and finally, "in the morning, a great while before day, he rose and went out to a lonely place, and there he prayed" (Mark 1:35). People saw God in Jesus' untiring response to others' need and in the graciousness of his words. The writer of the Fourth Gospel comments, "For God sent the Son into the world, not to condemn the world, but that the world might be saved through him." (John 3:17.)

God was incarnate in Jesus from the beginning of his life, and Jesus must early have accepted God's purpose for his life (which the story of the boy in the Temple tries to show, Luke 2:41-51). Although his gracious and sinless life was always showing forth the saving power of God toward men, this work was most fully known in the crucifixion and the resurrection.

Sin, man's separation from God which causes all wrongdoing, is serious. Man cannot live apart from the love of God, his Creator. The people of Israel tried in their national life to live apart from God who had chosen them, and they were overcome by their foes. This is the story told in The Book of Judges of the time when Israel was a federation of tribes. It is the story in the books of Isaiah and Jeremiah. It was the story of the individuals to whom Jesus spoke and to whom the apostles preached.

If sin were simply wiped out, there would be no justice. The Bible insists that God is the righteous One, so this is no possible solution in the light of the character of God. If sin remains, man cannot approach the holy God. Yet God will not have it thus, for he loves man. "I have loved you with an everlasting love; therefore I have continued my faithfulness to you." (Jer. 31:3.) Only God can overcome this separation.

Sin causes suffering. By becoming involved in that suffering, God indicates that he has taken the initiative.[5] Jesus sustained his relationship to God by his perfect obedience to God's purpose for his life, and showed that man could, by the power of God, live without sin. The Person of Jesus cannot be comprehended apart from his work. God's will to redeem man was one with Jesus' will to manifest that purpose in the world. The whole of Jesus' life was his self-giving for man. The climax of that life was the crucifixion. This is the awesome wonder before which man must be silent. Here was utter defeat and deepest shame. Here good was overcome by evil; love was overcome by hate.

That one person should suffer for another is not unknown. Whenever one person continues to love another who has caused suffering, that love can have a redemptive influence on the relationship and on the person causing the suffering. But the suffering of Jesus was more than martyrdom. It has been the experience of Christians through the years that his sufferings, becoming a present reality to them personally, redeemed their lives and made it possible for them to offer redemptive love to others. The Christian community has always had at its center persons who testified that Christ had redeemed them and who, for that reason, acknowledged him to be their Lord. This is because God's work was not completed on the cross: it was completed in the resurrection. This is what the Fourth Gospel interprets as the exaltation of Christ. " And I, when I am lifted up from the earth, will draw all men to myself." (John 12:32.)

If the cross had been the end of the story, evil would have triumphed, even though Jesus might have moved many by his example and his sacrifice. The resurrection affirmed that God was Lord over sin and death. This event drew the scattered disciples together and gave them the good news to preach. Death was not the end.

The resurrection was an experience shared only by the faithful. They had not expected it, but their lives were reoriented because of it. This affirmation seems incredible to those outside the household of faith. Not many years after the event, Paul wrote to the church at Corinth:

> " For the word of the cross is folly to those who are perishing, but to us who are being saved it is the power of God. . . .
> For Jews demand signs and Greeks seek wisdom, but we preach Christ crucified, a stumbling-block to Jews and folly to Gentiles, but to those who are called, both Jews and Greeks, Christ the power of God and the wisdom of God. For the foolishness of God is wiser than men, and the weakness of God is stronger than men." (I Cor. 1:18, 22-25.)

THE WORK OF THE HOLY SPIRIT

While the crucifixion and the resurrection were historic events, occurring at a particular time and place, their effects have been made known continuously in the world through the Christian community as the work of the Holy Spirit. The church's understanding of this work may be found in the words of the Fourth Gospel:

> "Nevertheless I tell you the truth: it is to your advantage that I go away, for if I do not go away, the Counselor will not come to you; but if I go, I will send him to you. And when he comes, he will convince the world of sin and of righteousness and of judgment: of sin, because they do not believe in me; of righteousness, because I go to the Father, and you will see me no more; of judgment, because the ruler of this world is judged." (John 16:7-11.)

The promise of the Holy Spirit (Acts, ch. 1) and the coming of the Spirit (Acts, ch. 2) immediately precede the proclamation of the gospel.

The work of the Holy Spirit enables the individual to respond to this proclamation which the Christian community makes and to understand that God has entered into human life through Jesus Christ, seeking to turn men's lives to a new relationship with himself. When a person realizes that he would have participated in crucifying the Son of God and that his kind of living continues the crucifixion, he sees himself in a new light and knows that he sins. He is not in relationship with God; rather, he is in opposition to God, in an inverted relationship. He wants most of all to fulfill his own ambitions and to perfect his own life, at whatever cost to himself or to others. In repenting he has turned around to face God. In judging himself he has known that he is judged, and then he knows also that God loves and forgives him. The cross that convicts him of sin simultaneously reveals to him the fullness of the love of God. Beyond the cross he sees the living Christ, assuring him that "'Death is swallowed up in victory.' . . . The sting of death is sin, and the power of sin is the law. But thanks be to God, who gives us the victory through our Lord Jesus Christ" (I Cor. 15:54, 56-57).

The "turning around," with its new direction for life, must appear at a particular point, but the work of the Holy Spirit continues for life. The preceding work is called, in theological language, " regeneration." The continuous work is known as " sanctification." This is the point at which some Christian groups fail, although they may have known the joy of the new life. They assume that regeneration brings automatic and immediate sanctification. They are beyond all law and they can do no wrong. That is a static point of view. Rather, the Holy Spirit is the living, present power of God continuing his saving work day by day in those whom he has called through Christ into the fellowship of his church. Nels F. S. Ferré writes:

" The Spirit of God urges both to self-being, i.e., to freedom and individuality, and to otherness, that is, to altruism and fellowship. We are genuine beings, not in spite of the presence of God in this wise, but precisely because of it. Similarly we are authentic persons when the Holy Spirit unites our self-drive into acceptance of self with others on a new level of freedom, precisely because of his presence." [6]

The Holy Spirit can transform every area of life and make it new. Because of this work, the apostle Paul can say, " We know that in everything God works for good with those who love him " (Rom. 8:28). " Spiritus Creator " describes God present and active in the lives of persons, uniting them with Christ and with one another in the fellowship of the church. He is the bond uniting the Creator with his creatures, bringing human wills into glad surrender to the purposes of the holy God.

But the work of the Holy Spirit cannot be completed in the span of earthly life. God had raised Jesus from the dead, and " as in Adam all die, so also in Christ shall all be made alive " (I Cor. 15:22). The resurrection of Jesus gave assurance to those who already believed in him. The return of Jesus would not of itself have convinced the skeptical, as Luke's Gospel indicates in the parable of the rich man and Lazarus. " He said to him, ' If they do not hear Moses and the prophets, neither will they be convinced if some one should rise from the dead.' " (Luke 16:31.)

The vision of some ultimate perfect society is no substitute, for progress is not necessarily inevitable, and there may quite possibly be a literal end to the world and all man's striving. Again, one might bravely dismiss the need for eternal life in regard to one's own existence, but it is quite another matter to imagine extinction for another person, whom one most loves.

The Christian affirmation of eternal life is rooted in the Christian understanding about God. As the love of God had been made known to the disciples in Christ and they had fellowship with him through the Holy Spirit, they were assured that this kind of existence would be even more perfectly realized after death. When they apprehended the fact that Jesus had died for them, they participated in his sufferings and knew also that they were already sharing in the eternal life which he gives. "If we have died with him, we shall also live with him," says the writer of Second Timothy (ch. 2:11). Paul writes, "If the Spirit of him who raised Jesus from the dead dwells in you, he who raised Christ Jesus from the dead will give life to your mortal bodies also through his Spirit which dwells in you." (Rom. 8:11.)

There is a strongly ethical note to the New Testament assurance of eternal life. It is a life with the holy God. There is no note of exclusion, and no word of how God, who desires not the death of a sinner, will accomplish the regeneration of those who seemingly have preferred to live and die apart from him. Yet there is no coercion in love, and God would not force this relationship upon those who have rejected him.

The incompleteness of human life and love is overcome by this assurance of eternal life. God who created man in his image and who sent his Son for man's redemption cares about each person. When a child dies young, or a young man falls in battle, or lovers are separated by death during the first years of their marriage, Christian faith has always affirmed that God is the Lord of life and with him there is no death.

Here, then, is the content of Christian nurture. Through the worshiping community God has made known his saving work for men in the life, death, and resurrection of his Son Jesus Christ. This work, once accomplished on Calvary and in its aftermath, is made immediate through the ever-present action of the Holy Spirit, who day by day continues to bring repentance and grace to those who are being saved in order that they may be strengthened in their relationship toward God and enabled to show forth the new life in Christ as a testimony before all the world. The consummation of this work awaits eternal life beyond the confines of the mortal body.

We have gone into considerable detail concerning this total theological orientation. It seems both desirable and necessary to remember the dynamic content of the Christian faith as we proceed to the development and reconstruction of the church's educational work, especially in the contemporary situation when even we who are in the church have sometimes neglected our real theological foundations.

But there is still another question to be faced before we are ready to address ourselves to problems of method and curriculum: Who are the persons to whom the good news is to be addressed? The next chapter will deal with that equally pivotal question.

4

Persons and Communication

The Human Need

D. M. Baillie points out that "in the modern world it is often said that the besetting question about the Christian faith or about any statement of it is not 'Is it true?' but 'Is it relevant?'"[1] As we have seen, the Christian faith and experience are grounded in the historical action of God made known through the event of Jesus Christ and first attested to by the early Christian community. As such it has an objective validity of its own and each reinterpretation must be seen in this context. It is still true, however, that every generation must understand its own deepest needs and the bearing that this gospel has on those needs. The analysis of man's present situation has been approached from many angles. Only by seeing these several facets can one have the totality in clear focus.

Often the aesthetic approach catches the spirit of the times more clearly than does a more prosaic word. In the crashing chords of atonal music, with its emphasis on sounding brass, one can feel the frustrations of an impersonal civilization's exploding. In non-melodic orchestrations one catches something of the meaninglessness which finds in music neither an expression of deep emotion nor a response to it.

Turning to the world of art one ponders surrealism, the mechanistic canvases, and the geometric designs of nonobjective painting. These seem to say that human existence is senseless, or bizarre, or merely routine. Man is an object set in the midst of his environment. When one finds a human face in a painting, it is likely to show the debauchery of war or the deprivation of famine, and middle-class figures reflect the irony with which the artist draws them. This is a far cry from the warm sensuousness that glows from a Renaissance goddess or the comforting beatitude in the eyes of a medieval Madonna.

Reference is often made to T. S. Eliot's phrase, "The Waste Land," the title of his long poem, and to "The Age of Anxiety," similarly used by W. H. Auden. A mood thus descriptive of our contemporary situation is found in much recent poetry, such as Karl Shapiro's description of the tourist visiting the cathedral at Washington, D.C.: "He is only a good alien; nominally happy." [2] There are the novels of Franz Kafka, as in the frantic meaninglessness of *The Trial,* where something ominous is happening but one can never quite pinpoint why it is happening, or how, or by whom — except that the book ends with the finality of the real death of a human being.

Then there is the sociological view of the situation. One book catches the feeling-tone of a large American factory, where any possible sense of community and individuality must take place within a small working group in one corner of the building.[3] The author describes the expressions of individuality and the attempts at maintaining a group solidarity, the lines along which these divide into subgroups, and the areas in which the men form a team. *Fortune,* magazine of the businessman, published a number of articles which analyzed the various facets of human existence within the framework of the business world.[4] These describe the way in which the corporation seeks to adjust the young executive and his family into its overarching purposes. The mores of suburbia are viewed; alarm is expressed at what is called "groupthink."

Philosophy has set as its task the probing of the depths of such environmental descriptions of man's existence in any given period. Logical positivism seeks to do this by compartmentalizing experience. Admitting that words lead to obfuscation as often as to clarity, the positivist seeks a vocabulary for each area of existence. His method is to find meaning according to categories. This has the value of insisting that not all areas of man's understanding can be studied from the same point of view.

Existentialism views man's life from the standpoint of "existence" and "being." It looks at existence phenomenologically, seeing life in terms of living and time in terms of experience. The fundamental concern is the concrete situation of people. Because it is a revolt against systematization, it can often best be seen through the novel or the drama. "The essence of man is his existence" is Jean-Paul Sartre's famous phrase.[5] Man's freedom is stressed — a freedom so utter that man's essential life is one of loneliness. He is "thrown" into existence. Each person is a threat to the identity of other persons. Such a freedom brings hopelessness. What is more, man knows not whence he comes, but he seems sure that the end of life is nothingness. He lives in constant anxiety because of his freedom and his mortality. Theistic existentialism, as seen particularly in Gabriel Marcel, sets man's existence in the framework of the personal God, in surrender to whom man has truest freedom.[6] Existentialist writing shows deep awareness of man's concern over his immediate situation, but often envisages the only possible solution to be within himself and the narrow confines of his present existence. By excluding even the possibility of interaction with other persons, it ends with a bare statement that man is, with no sense of purpose through his freedom or his existence.

In the United States an acceptable way of interpreting man's situation is made through the medium of psychology. No analysis of human existence would be complete without reference to the prevailing psychologies. Much of present-day psychology has its roots in the work of Sigmund Freud, with his disclosure of the hiddenness of man's essential motives and responses. The work of Freud's pupils continues in the work of *their* pupils, and today various offshoots of psychoanalysis find wide acceptance in the American scene. These have their place both in medical therapy and in educational theory and practice.

The depth psychologist, like the philosopher, sees guilt and anxiety at the root of individual existence, and he sees their results in various forms of hostility, expressed or repressed. Some believe that man has a drive toward self-destruction which only love can overcome. Others insist on the innate goodness of man and seek to build on that a humanistic ethic. In another view, man is understood in terms of his relationships with other persons. Guilt and anxiety are implied in all these points of view, whether positively or negatively expressed. A socio-psychological approach to the same problem is found in the writings of Kurt Lewin, who, through Gestalt psychology and psychoanalysis, elucidates the place of forces and patterns within the psychical and interpersonal environment in the development of hostility and submission.[7]

The child, like the adult, is deeply influenced by the emotional climate of the home and by the personalities of significant persons in his environment. If at various times and under varying circumstances the surrounding adults are anxious, he too becomes anxious. If such anxiety causes self-concern, the child is deprived of love. If it results in hostilities, the child does not feel acceptance. When it shows itself in forms of worry, the child is denied security. Moreover, psychologists emphasize the fact that the roots of many adult neuroses are to be found in childhood. It seems as though one is caught in a vicious circle. This week's headlines may report on widespread adolescent drinking. Last year's headlines were concerned with the adolescent use of drugs.

The child psychologists have uncovered some significant factors in children's lives. They are concerned about how the lovelessness and the repressions that beset many children are disturbing and distorting growing personalities. While still exploring areas of children's needs, they see the importance of the child's being accepted as a unique individual. Each child is himself and no one else. All children face a series of developmental tasks which must be accomplished at the individual's rate of maturation. Emotional security is the undergirding environment necessary for this work of growth, which includes bringing emotions into the pattern of living, accepting one's sex, learning the customs of society, and creating a self-image. Tensions and resentments develop early as the infant is fitted into a social pattern, but growth continues as a child receives loving guidance within the security of a stable situation and dependable human relations.

In summary it may be said that in current secular thinking man's situation is described as one of anxiety expressed through hostility, and his need is for a childhood marked by love, security, and acceptance.

The theological inquiry into man asks why he is anxious and why he needs to be told to love his children. Several writers have sought a psychological understanding of what Christian theology is trying to say. The important viewpoint shared by psychotherapists and contemporary theologians is a dynamic view of man and his life. Man is not an "object," philosophy is not a system, a way of life is not an ideal, and God is not a concept.

Other writers are concerned with a Biblical understanding of the human situation within the context of the theology of the church. The Bible begins, in the first chapter of Genesis, with the statement that God made man in his own image, and called all his creation good.

"Then God said, 'Let us make man in our image, after our likeness.' . . . So God created man in his own image, in the image of God he created him; male and female he created them. And God blessed them. . . . And God saw everything that he had made, and behold, it was very good." (Gen. 1:26-28, 31.)

That is the first thing to be said about the theological understanding of man. The "image of God" is taken to mean that man is not body alone, but also spirit, and in Hebraic thought the two were not separated as in Greek thought. Being spirit, man could respond to God, who is spirit; being person, he could know God, who is personal.

However, this must not be taken to mean that man is the equal of God. God is man's Creator and not vice versa. Man is always the creature. He derives existence from God and is wholly dependent upon God. His very freedom is not an innate quality of his humanity, but is itself a gift of God, his Creator. One of the implications of the myth of the Garden of Eden is that man has the freedom to choose obedience or disobedience, good or evil, God's purpose or man's ambition.

There is a paradoxical element in the Christian understanding of man which cannot be simplified or explained away. It is an indication of the fact that no human decision is ever "black or white." Thus it may be affirmed that while man does not have to sin, nevertheless he will sin. Man's finiteness is not evil, but it is that element in his existence which makes him dependent upon God. When he becomes anxious about his mortality, he becomes estranged from God and tempted to sin. Jesus counseled against anxiety, pointing out that God who takes care of the birds of the air and the flowers of the field will take care of his children. (See Matt. 6:25-34.)

Man seeks to overcome the insecurity caused by the knowledge of his finiteness through the development of pride. He develops a will to power. He pretends that he is not limited. ("Difficult things we do immediately; the impossible takes a little longer.") The end result of such personality development is that man puts himself in the place of God. He regards himself as self-sufficient. The only god he knows is the one he can imagine, and there is no point in worshiping one's own creation. Moreover, since he is himself the highest point in creation, the power of judgment belongs to him and he proceeds to use it against his fellows. His fellows, under such judgment, develop repressions and aggressions; realizing that they also judge him, he develops similar symptoms. Estrangement from God the Creator brings anxiety, which is compensated for through pride, which results in self-righteousness, self-love, and the love of things. This does not have to be so. Man is free to transcend his environment and to transcend himself in order to respond to God who seeks him.

In this analysis of man's situation and his need, it would seem that there are fundamental similarities among the viewpoints of art, philosophy, psychology, and theology. Man is anxious, guilty, and alone. He needs love, security, and acceptance — in Paul

Tillich's phrase, "the courage to be." It is in the solution of the problem that the differences become apparent. Jesus said, "Those who are well have no need of a physician, but those who are sick; I have not come to call the righteous, but sinners to repentance." (Luke 5:31-32.)

The "sickness unto death" evidently was as apparent in the first century of our era as in the nineteenth or the twentieth. It is to this situation that the good news addresses itself. God the Creator has made himself known as the Redeemer, coming to share in mortal existence, enduring suffering, degradation, and death. Overcoming all these, he offers to man a new life in relationship to himself through his Son Jesus Christ, and by the power of his Holy Spirit within the community of those who are being redeemed, the church. God's love has reached down to man's finitude to overcome man's pride; God's saving power in the Holy Spirit has offered man eternal life.

COMMUNICATION BETWEEN GOD AND MAN

The church tries to relate persons to God so that he may be accomplishing his saving work in them. This relationship is elicited in terms of communication. It is not enough to have an outline of what man needs and an understanding of what God offers him. These personal factors must be brought together before God's saving work can be done in and for man. Communication is a problem in all areas of existence today. The contemporary study of semantics is an effort to increase communication through an understanding of the deeper meaning of words. Each area of human knowledge has a particular vocabulary; sometimes one word has a different meaning in each of two fields of study. If men can say the same words and still not understand each other, no communication is established. The contemporary study of group dynamics is another effort to help understanding. Studies of how groups function indicate that communication is inhibited by blockages within personalities. People withdraw from one another, or they express hostility and aggressiveness. An understanding of the forces within a group situation is seen as a way of creating an accepting situation in which people will communicate with one another.

These understandings enter into the communication of the gospel. This is more than a matter of improving techniques or of finding out what people want in order that such needs may be supplied. There are pressures surrounding life today that militate against response. Although people are always among crowds, there is anonymity rather than recognition. Although science has attempted to bring the light of knowledge to replace ignorance, it has succeeded, seemingly, in bringing the new fear of mass annihilation. Out of these factors has developed an indifference toward moral standards and a general tendency to consider all ethics to be relative. The Christian gospel may be heard, but often it does not seem important. Yet the basis for human communication is the " word," and at the heart of the communication between God and man is the Word. This Word is most fully communicated through Jesus Christ. Communication has taken place when a person so far understands the gospel as to make a definite decision to respond to its call or to reject it.

Communication involves participation. The person who seeks to share the gospel, whether it be in factory, suburb, or in a distant culture, needs to participate in the life of those to whom he goes (without completely identifying with it). He needs to have a singleness of purpose which can awaken response.

A basic book on the philosophy of communication is *I and Thou*, by Martin Buber.[8] The author points out that there are fundamentally two types of relationships in life: a person-to-person relationship (I-Thou) and a person-to-thing relationship (I-It). The person-to-thing relationship should signify the context of the world of objects in which alone persons can exist. Sometimes, however, persons treat one another as " it." The " thou " is not found by seeking, but by meeting. Moreover, the " I " grows because of this meeting with other persons and becomes more truly himself. It may be inferred from this book that the basic nature of communication is interpersonal.

Since God is the living God, he confronts man in person-to-person encounter. This understanding of the way in which God deals with man comes from the Bible. The psalmist writes:

" O Lord, thou hast searched me and known me!
Thou knowest when I sit down and when I rise up;
thou discernest my thoughts from afar.
Thou searchest out my path and my lying down,
and art acquainted with all my ways."
(Ps. 139:1-3.)

The Bible is filled with the accounts of such confrontation. When Adam hid in the garden, it is written, " But the Lord God called to the man, and said to him, ' Where are you? ' " (Gen. 3:9). In Exodus it is written, " When the Lord saw that he turned aside to see, God called to him out of the bush, ' Moses, Moses! ' And he said, ' Here am I ' " (Ex. 3:4). Here is the call of the prophet Amos:

" Then Amos answered Amaziah, ' I am no prophet, nor a prophet's son; but I am a herdsman, and a dresser of sycamore trees, and the Lord took me from following the flock, and the Lord said to me, " Go, prophesy to my people Isreal." Now therefore hear the word of the Lord.' " (Amos 7:14-16.)

Such a meeting with the living God changes all of life. By seeing himself in relation to the Eternal One, man understands the true norm for his existence.

One should note also that this call of God is always a specific one, addressed to a particular person. Isaiah was in the Temple, meditating on the troublous times of his people, in the year that King Uzziah died. When he heard the seraphim call to one another, his instant response was: " Woe is me! For I am lost; for I am a man of unclean lips, and I dwell in the midst of a people of unclean lips; for my eyes have seen the King, the Lord of hosts! " And when he had made the personal response to the call of God, he was sent to be God's messenger to his people. (See Isa., ch. 6.) To be known of Him and called by one's name is the deepest assurance of security and the firmest foundation for every hope in life.

The way by which God makes himself known is called "revelation." This word, in its rootage, means to set aside the veil, and connotes making something clear or plain. There is a distinction between discovery and revelation, although in the archaic meaning of "discover" there is also implied revealing or disclosing. In our present usage of the word, we imply that a person discovers something by his own seeking, whereas a revelation is made to him by another person. Such a revelation may be factual information, although there is little such information that a person could not eventually discover for himself. The only revelation that has a unique character is the revelation of a self to another person. One can learn all *about* another person through discovery: reading his books, talking with his friends, and speaking with him. But a knowledge *of* the person can be had only from him, and only as he chooses to make himself known. No person can be persuaded to give this knowledge to another; it is given only in order to have a personal relationship; it is granted only because of love. Revelatory knowledge may be had between parent and child, husband and wife, friend and friend.

Since God is personal, knowledge of him must be in personal terms and must come from him. Man does not "discover" God, although he may discover objective facts about God. The knowledge of God through his world would be called "general" revelation. This is not "knowing" God as the Bible speaks of knowing him. The knowledge of God comes only by the gracious action of God himself as he seeks to make himself known to his children in love.[9] Because God has personally shown himself as love, one is able to look at the world and call it good. One can live without fear, knowing that the world was created by a righteous God and is sustained by him.

The self-disclosure of God has a moral dimension. A man must be changed before he can know God; he is faced with a demand that calls for acceptance with his whole life. This was the experience of Moses, Isaiah, Peter, and Paul. Yet the basic purpose of revelation is not demand, but love. Man uses his freedom to live his life apart from God, and the result is unhappiness and frustration because one is cut off from the source of true existence. God in his love and mercy seeks to make himself known to man, and when man realizes that the Holy One has drawn near, he is able to apprehend the moral demand.

Man's response to revelation may be called " appropriation." Since God is not an idea, and his revelation is not an abstract " truth," man's response cannot be in intellectual terms alone. The self-giving of God can be met only by the response of the whole man. Love must be met by love. The holiness of God calls forth the moral purpose of man. If there were only knowledge about God, knowledge that man could discover, there would be no need for urgency or decision. It could be filed away in the mind with other factual knowledge, and would have no real meaning in terms of life.

But the self-disclosure of God is not like that. When man receives and accepts the love of God, there comes about a changed relationship. He is not his own: he freely gives his allegiance to God, whom he now sees as his Creator and his Redeemer. His life has a new center in God, and a new purpose: to serve God. Accepting the freedom wherewith God created him, man has now bound himself and has thereby become most free. In the opening sentence of his letter to the Romans, Paul writes that he is " a servant [or slave] of Jesus Christ " (Rom. 1:1). The situation is put even more dramatically in the first Corinthian letter:

> " Were you a slave when called? Never mind. But if you can gain your freedom, avail yourself of the opportunity. For he who was called in the Lord as a slave is a freedman of the Lord. Likewise he who was free when called is a slave of Christ. You were bought with a price; do not become slaves of men. So, brethren, in whatever state each was called, there let him remain with God." (I Cor. 7:21-24.)

The possibility of being both slave and free at the same time is not a matter that can be analyzed and synthesized, but it is nonetheless an experience to which Christians have always testified.

Appropriation, which causes a changed relationship between

man and God, results in a new way of life; indeed, in newness of life itself. Paul's experience led him to relate:

> "I have been crucified with Christ; it is no longer I who live, but Christ who lives in me; and the life I now live in the flesh I live by faith in the Son of God, who loved me and gave himself for me." (Gal. 2:20.)

Every expression of response to the gospel in love and service to all people through the community of the church is the result of this appropriation. The gospel becomes communicated through the testimony of word and action that the church makes in the world as it seeks to bring the world to God in Christ.

The revelation that results in appropriation is made possible by the grace of God. The word for " grace " has sometimes been translated in the Revised Standard Version of the Bible as " favor." Thus in Ps. 84:11: "For the Lord God is a sun and shield; he bestows favor and honor." In The Acts of the Apostles and in the epistles, the terms " the grace of God " or " the grace of the Lord Jesus Christ " take on depth of meaning. " They are justified by his grace as a gift." (Rom. 3:24.)

The grace of God, as understood in the Bible, is not an abstraction, but is known through its work in men. This is the graciousness of God by which he draws men unto himself and wins them from self-centeredness into a life of fellowship with himself through Christ. It is therefore prior to man's response, although its acceptance lies in the turning of man toward God. The grace of God chooses man as his own; forgives his sins and makes him just; then sanctifies him daily through the Holy Spirit. The grace of God is made known through his provision for human life in the world and by the constant renewal of the goodness of life. In the Protestant understanding, grace is not a mechanical power, although it may be apprehended in power. It is rather a dynamic quality known in a life committed to God. It was by grace that Paul recognized Jesus as the Christ. It was by grace that the Holy Spirit indwelt the fellowship of the church, and indwells it still. Because God loves, he is gracious in every action. He could not act other than graciously toward those whom he has made, yet he has given them freedom to reject his grace in order that their response might be freely made. While it has seemed to some that this view compromises the sovereignty of God, it is answered that his sovereignty is not one of power but of love, and it is exercised in the sphere of personal relationships. There is a compulsive power to love which is not mechanical, just as there is to fact and to truth. Grace has moral implications, for it is the work of the holy God toward those who are serving him. Grace is more than human love, for it proceeds from the eternal God as a way of his communication with men. It is the basis for the personal relationship with his children which he has established through Jesus Christ by the Holy Spirit within the fellowship of the church.

Man's response to grace is called faith. God, who has revealed himself to men graciously in love, thereby evokes the commitment of the whole self. This involves a reorientation of life whereby God and not man is the center of existence. God is now seen to be the Creator and the source of life. He is known through Christ as the one who has acted to save man from aloneness, anxiety and despair, sin and death. His gracious activity is known in the ordering of life. When this is comprehended and appropriated by the total life of a person, he has no fear. This is no leap into the dark; it is not blind belief. Those who have seen God in the face of Jesus Christ know in whom they have believed, and understand him in whom they put their trust. Such assurance was known in the Old Testament. " When I am afraid, I put my trust in thee." (Ps. 56:3.) This is paralleled by the witness to the faithfulness of God, as in Ps. 119:90: " Thy faithfulness endures to all generations."

Faith, in the New Testament, takes on a new dimension. A glance at the columns of a standard concordance will indicate this fact. The word of Hab. 2:4, " The righteous shall live by his faith," enriched by the experience of Paul, became the basis for all the depth of meaning that this word has contained for Christians. Discovered anew by Martin Luther in his Greek New Testament, it became the burning word of the Reformation; and Luther's commentary on Romans, read by John Wesley, became in turn the key for the release of his life to the power of God.

This is "saving faith," by which a person knows that his sin is forgiven, that God has accepted him in a new relationship and will sustain him with the power for righteous living. One does not do good in order to be forgiven; one is forgiven in order to do good.

> "But God, who is rich in mercy, out of the great love with which he loved us, even when we were dead through our trespasses, made us alive together with Christ (by grace you have been saved), and raised us up with him, and made us sit with him in the heavenly places in Christ Jesus, that in the coming ages he might show the immeasurable riches of his grace in kindness toward us in Christ Jesus. For by grace you have been saved through faith; and this is not your own doing, it is the gift of God — not because of works, lest any man should boast. For we are his workmanship, created in Christ Jesus for good works, which God prepared beforehand, that we should walk in them." (Eph. 2:4-10.)

This faith response is made to the proclamation of God's work through the gospel as the church testifies to it by life and word. Faith, shown in loving, trustful obedience to the purposes of God, is the way in which man testifies to what God has done for him. This faith is sustained and nourished within the fellowship of the worshiping community through every activity of the church: prayer and preaching, the hearing of the Scriptures, the partaking of the sacrament, and works of service. Faith is God's gift, appropriated by man in the totality of his life, that he may live in everlasting fellowship with his Creator and Redeemer.

The relationship between God and man finds its expression in prayer. The Bible records such relationship. There is the story of Abraham, chosen as the ancestor for God's elect people; Moses, pleading for the wayward children of the promise; the prophets, protesting their high calling yet yearning for their people's salvation. The letters of Paul are filled with his prayers for the people of the churches. Jesus was sustained by prayer from his temptation in the wilderness to his last cry on the cross.

Prayer involves faith in a living, personal God who is immediately present and with whom one can have fellowship. Friedrich Heiler ends his historical study with the conclusion that the essence of prayer is petition.[10] The I-Thou relationship is preserved here, for to ask is to receive a reply. There can be no abstract sense of wonder, no losing oneself in the universal, where petition is involved. Only God as person can hear and answer. Only where there is a personal relationship of love and trust is there the freedom to ask and to receive. He to whom God is known as Father cannot do other than pray according to his need. Jesus first prayed, "Abba, Father, all things are possible to thee; remove this cup from me"; and he concluded, "Yet not what I will, but what thou wilt." (Mark 14:36.) [11]

Not only is one to pray, but he is also to expect an answer. How God answers prayer is something that only he, in his love and wisdom, knows. That he answers prayer is the affirmation of all who have lived with him in the I-Thou relationship. Such prayer is an expression of trust and is part of the response of faith. In the gospel stories people are never seen to petition Jesus in vain. Whatever they ask in faith they receive. Jesus' teaching about prayer concerns petition. He gives the example of a man who goes to a friend at night asking for bread for a visitor. Then he continues: "Ask, and it will be given you; seek, and you will find; knock, and it will be opened to you. For every one who asks receives, and he who seeks finds, and to him who knocks it will be opened." (Luke 11:9-10.)

Such prayer includes every need of man for himself and for others — individual need and social necessity. The church on earth and the church in heaven are bound together by their mutual life of prayer, through Christ, who even while on earth forgave the sins of men; and by the Holy Spirit, who alone gives the power to pray in harmony with the purposes of God for his people, his church, and his world.

Praise is central to prayer; not merely as admiration of God's works, but as an activity of the whole self, at all times to God's glory. The psalmist says, "I will bless the Lord at all times; his praise shall continually be in my mouth." (Ps. 34:1.) Thanksgiving is essentially an enumeration of the acts of God in praise and gratitude. "Praise the Lord. I will give thanks to the Lord with my whole heart. . . . He has caused his wonderful works to be remembered. . . . He sent redemption to his people." (Ps. 111:1, 4, 9.)

These are the ways in which God confronts man in order to have communication with him. God, who is personal, and who has been known as a person in Jesus Christ, reveals himself to man and seeks him by his gracious love in order that man might respond in faith and appropriate God's purposes into the totality of his life. Prayer is the expression of this encounter through which man asks and God gives within this personal relationship.

Persons as Channels of Communication

Those who have found a new relationship to God (through Christ, within the fellowship of the church) find also a new relationship with one another. They are removed from the status of being impersonal entities toward one another. Each becomes more fully a person because of what he receives from and gives to the lives of other persons. The church then can be truly the redemptive community.

As a result, those outside the church, seeing the meaning for persons, are drawn into its orbit by their need. They enter into a situation in which they are ready to hear the *kērygma* and respond to its gracious message. This response would be of little avail if the standards of the community into which the new Christians were brought should be the same as those of the environment they were leaving. But the church, made up of those who are drawn together by what God has done for them in Christ, can draw others into a new relationship with God and with one another. The anonymity of the transportation system and the insecurity of the market place are overcome. "In the world you have tribulation; but be of good cheer, I have overcome the world." (John 16:33.) The relationship of persons to

God and one another within the church makes possible the living of life in subway and market place.

Those who have experienced this transformation within the church are enabled to mediate God's redemptive influence in the other relationships of their lives. The closest of these relationships is that of marriage. Those who have known the love of God are enabled to love one another. Marriage becomes a channel through which each person grows because of a life lived with another person, in love and not merely in proximity. Such a domestic relationship provides a foundation on which children can grow, secure in love and acceptance.

The experience of a gracious relationship with God transforms the other areas of man's everyday existence, enabling him to be a channel for influencing interpersonal patterns in social and economic groups and to know when existent patterns must be accepted and endured in a redemptive spirit. This is operative wherever there are tensions or strife, in business life or community affairs; in racial, political, or economic problems; in national or international affairs. God is the Lord over all his creation, and the power of the cross has not diminished with the centuries.

But all faithful members of the church know that this really does not happen. Their personal lives and the life of the Christian community have not been that completely transformed! There is friction even within the everyday work of a parish. There are tensions even in the most loving families. There are forces of evil abroad in the social, economic, and political life of mankind which seem to overwhelm the best hopes of devout believers. This realization keeps the church from any illusion of seeming perfect. There is no answer that will solve this problem. Because the church is composed of human beings living in the world, the Kingdom (Kingship) of God cannot be perfectly realized in their midst. One seeks to do good, and evil results. One is asked to choose "between two evils." One is involved, as was the Lord of the church in his earthly life, with the sins of the world.

Particular persons may become channels of communication for

the gospel in particular ways. God speaks to the committed individual, through whom he makes his purpose known as he did of old by prophets and apostles. Martin Luther was used by God to bring fresh springs of life into the church, and John Wesley brought the warmth of the gospel anew into eighteenth-century England. Each in his own way and according to his own time was a reformer, and each had a unique place in the purpose of God to chastise and to revive his church.

The *kērygma* is not static, nor is the fellowship. " God has yet more light to break forth from his holy word " is the much-quoted dictum of the Pilgrim pastor John Robinson of Leyden. This light often breaks through the committed individual, nourished in the life of the church. Augustine gave a new direction to the Western church after the fall of Rome and thereby set the course for more than a thousand years. John Calvin clarified the understandings of the Reformation in an outline that has become basic for succeeding centuries.

The church communicates the gospel in terms of personal encounter, to develop committed individuals who become in turn channels of communication. The missionary is one of these as he participates in the life of those to whom he is sent, in order that through sympathetic understanding he may testify to what God has done for him, and can do, through his redeeming love. The transformed person testifies to what God has done for him not only by his words, but in his life, through kindness, understanding, and good works. Outsiders are thereby drawn toward the community of the church.

Such persons have a sense of vocation. They know that they are called by God in every moment of their life and in every area of their existence. Their daily work is his call and a channel through which they can be used by him for witnessing to the gospel. Their community life is his call to mediate the divine concern in the place where people live. Their family life is a call for growing relationships of love through which the Holy Spirit is in truth the Lord and the giver of life. Every person who comes to believe the good news does so because it has been mediated to him in his own situation by parents, teachers, ministers, and friends. What God does for a person is made known to other persons by him, and he thereby becomes a channel through whom God can speak to still others. Communication is in terms of personal relationships in which there is love and concern. There is no need for the fear which causes resistances and ego-building devices. God enables men to communicate not alone with himself but also with one another.

For several generations the findings of psychology have been eagerly sought as an aid to religious education. "Basic needs" and "developmental tasks" have become common parlance. That these "needs" are part of the total human environment has been less emphasized. The channels of communication which God has given through faith, grace, and prayer have been almost completely neglected in the orientations of most Protestants who have been concerned with the theory of Christian nurture. Here is a place where techniques fail and where persons — parents and fellow members in the church of Christ — must themselves be regarded as the profoundest media for communication.

Arriving at Methodology

MEDIA FOR COMMUNICATION

Not only has God desired relationship with his creatures; he has made ways by which men can know that this is so, and be drawn toward him. The fellowship of the church with its Lord is expressed through worship, and the form itself is expressive of communication. Worship consists of something that God does and the way by which men respond. God's action does not simply precede the service, but it is also to be found in the service. The component elements of the service become existential in so far as they are the response of the worshiping congregation to God's prior action and Christ's presence among his people.

The Creed, or confession, as the united testimony of the community within its own fellowship, grows out of worship and is an expression of worship. This confession was so radical an act in the early church that the catechumens were required to leave the service immediately preceding its recital. To this day the liturgy of the Eastern churches includes the sentence in which their departure is commanded. The Creed is Biblical in that its phrases derive from the words and experiences recorded in the New Testament, and are continuous with the simple, basic confessions of the apostolic church.

Hymnody is a musical expression of Biblical thought. The earliest hymns are the psalms. The hymns of the New Testament are confessional. The hymns of the Reformation reflect both the Biblical (Genevan Psalter) and the confessional (chorales) em-

phases. Modern hymnody is an expression of the existential situation of the worshiping community, whether it be known through
the emotion of the gospel hymns in pentecostal sects or the affirmations of a new social order in Protestant liberalism.

The church prays through the words of the Bible, the collects
of ancient liturgies, the phrases of Reformation prayer books, and
the needs of an immediate congregation. In this communication
God, who has addressed his people through the action heard in
Scripture, is addressed by them in praise and petition.

Teaching and preaching are a further part of communication.
Here the teacher or the preacher is the medium through whom
God makes himself known, and the word in Scripture is made
relevant to the needs of Christians in the church and in the world.
Thus the teacher or preacher is himself a witness and a part of
the situation.

All these elements of liturgy are rooted in the Bible and are
expressions of the Bible. The Bible belongs to the Christian community. Liturgy is a form of communication; the Bible is the
content of communication. For this reason it is important to
understand how the church looks at the Bible. A symposium by
scholars from various member groups of the World Council of
Churches evidences a high degree of mutual understanding concerning the Bible.[1] It is seen in its unity, existing as the medium
through which God speaks to man. This self-disclosure is understood in terms of his activity. In the Old Testament, this activity
was made known in the history of Israel. The creative and redemptive work of God reached a culmination in his action
recorded in the New Testament. Karl Barth gives a simple definition when he says, " The Bible is the concrete medium by which
the church recalls God's revelation in the past, is called to expect
revelation in the future, and is thereby challenged, empowered,
and guided to proclaim." [2]

The term " the word of God " expresses the fact of person-to-
person communication. In this sense it may be said that the Bible
contains the word of God, for in its words God speaks to men to
reveal himself. The word is personal and speaks to a particular

situation. It is concrete, yet not tangible. It does not force itself upon the hearer. The word of God in the Old Testament was the word that God spoke by the covenant, the law, and the prophets.

Contemporary theologians understand that the term "the word of God" is fulfilled most completely through God's self-disclosure in the Person of his Son Jesus Christ. Yet the Bible cannot be said to contain his word, for a person cannot be contained within the framework of descriptive words, even when these are his own words. The Bible points to Christ as the Word of God. This is the way in which it "contains" the Word.

This understanding comes by the testimony of the Holy Spirit, and has found classic expression in the writings of the founders of the Reformation. John Calvin says, for example:

> "For as God alone is a sufficient witness of himself in his own word, so also the word will never gain credit in the hearts of men, till it be confirmed by the internal testimony of the Spirit. It is necessary, therefore, that the same Spirit, who spake by the mouths of the prophets, should penetrate into our hearts, to convince us that they faithfully delivered the oracles which were divinely intrusted to them." [3]

To say merely that God spoke only through the Bible would be to make God's self-disclosure static. The Holy Spirit makes this record contemporaneous and thereby keeps it relevant to the life of the church. The reader receives interpretation according to his point of view. Some find it a valuable revelation of early Semitic historical records. Others have aesthetic pleasure in the measured cadences of the Psalter (especially in the King James Version). Some see it as a sociological record. Others are interested in its biographical content. Still others are impressed by its high moral code.

These are the varied backgrounds of understanding from which the question is asked, "How do believers see the Bible as the Word of God?" God himself, through his Holy Spirit, must so interpret the words of Scripture. Through this work, a person is enabled to appropriate that which he knows to be religiously true, and to respond in trust to God. The man of faith hears God's word in Scripture. The story of the walk to Emmaus expresses this insight, for the risen Christ expounded to these disciples the meaning of Scripture and was also made known to them in the breaking of bread. The Holy Spirit strengthens the church for the task of proclaiming the message.

The Bible — the written word of God's revelation; the Holy Spirit — the personal agent of God's revelation; and the church — the living community of testimony to God's revelation, bear witness to one another and interact with one another. God has given two dimensions through which he can be apprehended: faith and reason. God alone, and no written word about him, is the ultimate authority. The whole question of "authority" in any legalistic sense can only arise when the Bible is viewed as a series of precepts or a code of laws. What the Bible does for men is to witness to what God has done and the ways in which he has shown himself to his people. Its special task is to keep ever before the church his historic act of redemption in the life, death, and resurrection of Jesus Christ, in order that the church may proclaim this good news to all the world.

The Bible is a written word. This word is seen as action in the sacraments, of which Protestantism recognizes two as clearly commanded by Jesus: Baptism and the Lord's Supper. Baptism is the sacrament through which one enters into the Christian life. It is "foreshadowed" in the Old Testament rite of circumcision, which is connected with God's covenant of grace with his people Israel. Today, as in the primitive church, Baptism is the dramatic re-enactment through which the believer participates in the death and resurrection of the Lord and is thereby reborn into eternal life.

Infant baptism needs to be seen in this light. Admittedly its Biblical basis is indecisive. It arose as a practical necessity in the second generation of the church when Christian parents wanted their children to participate in the regenerative life of the church at an early age. The present concern, however, is with the place and meaning of infant baptism for the life of the child within the church.[4] Baptism derives its primary authentication through the fact that it is the seal of that which God has already done and the testimony of that which he will continue to do. A basic statement of this fact was made centuries ago in John Calvin's *Institutes of the Christian Religion*:

> " The children of believers are not baptized, that they may thereby be made the children of God, as if they had before been strangers to the Church; but, on the contrary, they are received into the Church by a solemn sign, because they already belonged to the body of Christ by virtue of the promise." [5]

Because of the redemptive work that God did in Christ, he is already at work by his Holy Spirit in every child who is born into the world, and he has given men ways by which they may participate in his work. Life in the community of the church is such a way. Baptism is the rite by which the church attests to the fact of God's saving grace and receives the child into the fellowship. He is surrounded by the love and care of its people and undergirded by the responsibility they bear for his growth in the Christian life. The prayer of the church is an important aspect of baptism, as indicated when the apostles at Jerusalem sent Peter and John to the group in Samaria who had been baptized but who had not yet received the gift of the Spirit. (See Acts 8:14-17.)

Baptism also is a reminder that the parents are a part of this covenant. They are the members of the church who have the particular responsibility for the child, because he is a gift of God to them and a responsibility from God. It is a part of their calling so to bring him up that in due time he will make his own confession of faith. The church gives the child an environment in which he is loved and accepted as a child of God; parents are given particular responsibilities because this is their child. Child, parents, and church are all connected in this action of God through baptism.

Above all, infant baptism is a testimony to the prevenient grace of God, seeking relationship with each of the children whom he has created. A child cannot show faith. He cannot ask for baptism. He cannot try in any way to prove his merit. He is literally brought to the font. There God says that he will ever sustain him by his grace and follow him with a love that never fails. This is assurance to the parents as well as a perpetual warning to the church that God is God.

While baptism is a once-and-for-all act by which the individual participates in the death and resurrection of the Lord, the Lord's Supper is the repeated celebration of this same fact. This activity gives the community an awareness of its solidarity. Preaching may be carried on in any place, and heard by all comers. Only within the church as the body of Christ is the sacrament observed and the Lord known as truly present in the midst of his people. The Lord's Supper always has this corporate character. "We who are many are one body, for we all partake of the same loaf." (I Cor. 10:17.)

This corporate act is also proclamation. "You proclaim the Lord's death until he comes." (I Cor. 11:26.) It is the dramatic form of the *kērygma* that makes the death and resurrection of Christ contemporaneous. Jesus made himself known to his disciples again and again through the breaking of bread: in the feeding of the multitude; at the home of friends, such as Peter, or Mary and Martha; in his eating with those whom he called, such as Levi and Zacchaeus. When the risen Lord met his disciples in the upper room or by the Lake of Galilee, he broke bread with them. There has never been any discontinuity in this way whereby Jesus has been known in his church. Not only in the night in which he was betrayed, but in the night of his resurrection and in the morning after the disciples had been fishing, and the nights and mornings throughout the centuries, he has shared this meal with those who by faith have confessed him Lord and Christ. Whether the church holds to transubstantiation, or consubstantiation, or some other affirmation of the Real Presence, this has always been the act of fellowship in which all believers could participate. It was not until the Reformation that within the liturgy the word in preaching was separated from the word in the sacrament. The unity of these two aspects of the liturgy is still maintained in the Eastern churches, the Roman Church, the Anglican churches, and in a denomination whose origins lie distinctively in America, the Disciples of Christ.[6] An increase in the frequency of celebrations of the Communion service is observable among Protestants,[7] and an emphasis on more frequent reception of Communion among Roman Catholics. The fellowship of the church derives from the fact that Christ the Lord is present in its midst. The church remembers this when its members sup with him.

There are four elements in the Lord's Supper: remembrance, sacrifice, fellowship (communion), and eucharist (thanksgiving). Through participation the worshiper finds sustaining power for his life in the world and a new assurance of the continuing activity of the Holy Spirit. It is a testimony of faith — preceded always by the recital of the Creed of which it is a re-enactment.

Sacraments are signs which God gives of his activity among men. They are visible and, in a sense, tangible, which makes them a means for expressing the inexpressible. They " say " what words cannot say. This is why they can be a unique medium for communication between God and man. The church has always grown in strength where the sacraments were honored and received by faith. Where they are neglected, faith may become coldly intellectualistic or vaguely mystical. By insisting that the material is real and good, created by God and used by him, they prevent dichotomy between body and spirit, substance and essence. They proclaim God through the familiar, yet they transmute the familiar into the ineffable. " The Word became flesh and dwelt among us." (John 1:14.) " This is my body, which is broken for you." (I Cor. 11:24, KJV.)

Connected with the Lord's Supper as a medium of communication and a way of proclamation from earliest times is Christian charity (*caritas*). The interrelationship between the two is seen in the *agapē* (love feast) of the early church and the primitive Supper, to which members brought food both for themselves and for others.

The Old Testament had urged kindness toward the stranger, but postexilic Judaism tended toward a legalistic interpretation of the Scriptures. In the Roman Empire of the first century, the regular provision for meeting the needs of the community, as practiced by Christians, was a new thing. The reality of a fellowship, which they possessed, had been virtually unknown in the ancient world. There were the family, the state, and the Empire, but none of these involved community. Religion was carried on by the priests in behalf of the people. Only within the household of faith could people experience fellowship. This fellowship, experienced intimately in the service of preaching, prayer, and Supper, was further made known in the concern that Christians felt toward one another.

Such concern was not a legal matter, arising from precept, but was the response of the community to their Lord. The reign of God would necessarily be one of love, for God is love, and only those dwell therein who have received his love into their hearts. All life is lived within this framework of love. It can neither be commanded by others nor developed by an individual within himself by much trying. It comes as the Holy Spirit illumines the words of Scripture regarding the loving work of God on Calvary and in the resurrection. The person who hears or reads is drawn to return that love and find fellowship within the community that made it known. Herein lies the motivation for Christian social action. It is the service of the whole person in order that others may become a part of the Kingdom and thereby be enabled to fulfill their vocation as sons of God.

The early Christians sought to make their lives a testimony to their faith. They were careful in their conduct toward others, seeking to live in gentleness and kindness with all people. Thus they hoped both to gain tolerance for themselves and to win others to Christ.

It is well known that the exercise of Christian love toward those outside the community, or even within it, has not always been shown in fullest measure. The giving of alms eventually became a rule. Christians are often urged by every propaganda device known through modern psychology to support the local church, and support of the church abroad has often been looked upon more with misgiving than with love. That may be part of the reason why the younger churches are themselves beginning to look doubtfully upon gifts from the West.

Yet the church still makes its witness to the world, testifying thereby that God wills to save all mankind and draw all people to himself in love. Loving service is a vital medium through which the gospel is communicated by action for the understanding of all men. Words require intellectual understanding. But acts of love can be apprehended by young and old, the sick and the dying, the bitter and the bewildered. In them, too, Christ is truly present among his people and seeks to make himself known to all mankind.

How the Church Teaches

The answer to men's need can come through the community of those who have received that answer into their lives. This is understandable in the twentieth century, for the era of individualism has been succeeded by a day in which people seek their security through the group. Contemporary trends in psychology agree. Psychoanalysis stresses the fact that the individual only knows himself as a person in so far as he can identify with and separate himself from surrounding persons. Gestalt psychology points out the importance of the total surroundings in learning. Field theories combine psychoanalysis and Gestalt to observe group interactions. Present philosophical understandings of persons as " subject " rather than as " object " emphasize the same theme. Karl Heim says that the " thou " can be approached " only if we give up all attempts to reduce it to a concept, to explain it causally, or to fit it into a system." He continues:

" In practical life we see this specific difference between the ' I-It ' world and the ' I-Thou ' relation more particularly in education and in psychotherapy. For the teacher, the pupil is an object of education, and therefore an ' it,' which he must study, must analyze, in order to understand better. . . . The pupil's behavior is explained first by the mental structure and psychology of a particular period of youth. Then account must be taken of the hereditary factors, race, family, and social grade, as well as of the influences of the age and the environment. But the pupil himself offers an invincible opposition to this analytical method which tries to fit him into some class or other. . . . He shuts himself up against being 'understood' in his fashion. He feels clearly that he is being treated as an object, an 'it.' The more virtuosity, subtlety, and experience displayed by the teacher in the application of this analytic method . . . the more hopeless this makes it to bring about a real meeting with the 'thou' of the pupil." [8]

The person as "thou" can best be appreciated in a context that is in its very essence personal. The church should be such a community.

The Christian community bases the assurance for teaching on the remembrance of how God has led and taught his people through all history. The church teaches through corporate worship. The way in which the church offers praise and prayer to God through Christ says something to all who participate. To the stranger, the inquirer, and the child this is a special way of teaching. It is not simply "learning by doing," for here the self is engaged at the deepest levels. Even a child can apprehend facets of what is happening in corporate worship. It is not certain what meanings this holds for him, and probably the meanings vary according to the child himself, his development, his family relationships, his linkages with the church, and his own relationship to God. Yet adults who remember attending the church service as children will recall the feeling-tone of the service, the meaning it seemed to hold for their family with whom they sat, the significance in the minister's face and voice. There could be apprehension without full comprehension.

Further teaching comes through the observance of the church year. This has a rhythm which brings order and pattern into the church's teaching. The cultural community has its holidays, but they follow one another in no perceptible order, save that of the calendar year. The church year begins at Advent, the weeks of preparation for the celebration of God's coming in Jesus Christ. This season goes into Epiphany: the manifestation of Christ to the world. Pre-Lent and Lent remind the church of the life of its Lord, while Passion Week brings the remembrance of the climactic event on Golgotha. The Easter festival which follows continues through Ascension Day and Pentecost. In less than six months, the church has remembered those acts of God which are the mainspring of its living faith. The remaining Sundays are the expression of the whole Christian understanding of God as Trinity.

The church year is an ordered expression of the *kērygma,* encompassing its wholeness from beginning to end. This was understood by those who, across the centuries, collected the liturgical materials found in the prayer books. At first sight, it is startling to turn to the traditional gospel for the first Sunday in Advent and read the story of the triumphal entry into Jerusalem. The epistle reads, "The night is far spent, the day is at hand." (Rom. 13:12, KJV.) This is the *kērygma;* here is an echo of the apostolic preaching. The gospel is a unity: the incarnation presages the crucifixion and the resurrection; the latter is the fulfillment of the event at Christmastide. It is impossible to celebrate the Nativity as a simple story of the birth of a baby. The outcome is already known, and the crib at Bethlehem signifies Emmanuel. The church has a rich resource for teaching as its people are enabled to follow week by week the recital of God's saving activity proclaimed in gospel and recreated within the framework of the Christian year.

The church also teaches through the relationships that exist between the adults and the children of the church. There are churches in which children do not feel accepted. This does not refer, necessarily, to the fact that their class meets in the kitchen, although that might be symptomatic of adult indifference. It refers to whether or not the adult members really enjoy having the children in their midst or whether the latter are merely tolerated. It is the difference between ignoring children in the building or greeting them and knowing them by name. It is not in the multitude of things that love is made known, but in the giving of the self.

There is no need to be sentimental on this subject. Children too are members of the community and as such have their responsibilities. Adults are not required to enjoy the interruptions of thoughtless children, although when thoughtlessness is due to immaturity, adults can find ways of changing the physical situation in such a way as to meet both the children's desires and their own. Members of the community, aware of their own constant need of the love and mercy of God, will be enabled to find such ways of living at peace with their younger members. A. Victor Murray has pointed out that one of the characteristics of the Christian community is that it is "a society of unlikes as well as of likes." This factor generates tensions. He comments:

> "Yet the Christian community is precisely a society of that kind, and the right word to use here is not 'overcome' but 'utilize.' For tension is the very breath of life to the Christian community, and a segregated society of likes is its negation. This fact is not always grasped, and in these days there is often too much segregation within the church — women's meetings, boys' clubs, girls' clubs, junior church, and so on. These have their essential place in the scheme of corporate life, but they can easily tend to avoid tension rather than to sublimate it. But part of religious education is to train people to live together in a society of difference. . . . Paul's implication is that 'in Christ' these distinctions are neither eliminated nor ignored but transcended." [9]

The church always remembers that the Lord set a child in the midst and said, "Whoever receives one such child in my name receives me" (Matt. 18:5). Correction within the church is always correction in love. Members accept one another as they are with the realization that this is not what they always will be. By the grace of God there is growth in Christian living as the members of the community uphold one another in love. Many children have known early in life what the fullness of Christian faith can mean because they have seen this in the faces and words and actions of a few adult Christians. This witness is a powerful word of God to children in each generation as they grow toward their time of commitment.

The church teaches through the church school. In the United States this means the Sunday church school, with additional teaching through weekday and vacation classes. The church school is a characteristic part of Christian education in the United States. It has survived for more than one hundred and fifty years, and it has taken on an increasing importance since the educational work for the cultural community became the responsibility of the state. Even parents who do not count themselves members of the church often wish their children to have a grounding in the Christian faith. While the word " school " has often connoted only formal instruction, the church school in the past few decades has broadened the meaning as has the cultural school.

The church teaches through the participation of children and adults in the total life of the Christian community. This happens whenever all work together and plan together. For example, a congregation chose to send a Lenten offering for a specific purpose and children saved money toward the goal along with the adults; or, a church was planning how to meet the needs of its neighbors, and children as well as adults gave their suggestions from the needs they knew about.

Biblical criticism, in seeing the unity of the Bible, in speaking of diversity rather than divergence, in re-creating the essential proclamation, and in affirming that the Bible is the written record of God who acts, has made it necessary for the church to ask whether all this is made known to the children. Every aspect of the church school is involved in this re-evaluation: the written curriculum, the enrichment materials, the methods, session procedures, worship, service activities, and the teacher's view of the task.

It is important that the church school shall always know itself to be a part of the church. The early Sunday schools did not meet in churches and were not a part of the churches' program. Many churches hesitated to admit the Sunday school. Organic unity of the church school within the life of the church is still far from fulfillment. This may be due in part to the emphasis on the church as an institution. In such a static understanding of the nature of the church, each part can become a separate entity. Indeed, there is an " itness " of relationship which hardly becomes the living body of Christ the Lord.

The church school is a way through which children are nurtured in the Lord. Children are not brought there primarily to learn right concepts or to be shown how to be good. According to his age, each child, already acknowledged a member of the church by baptism, is brought into the possibility of a relationship with God who loves him and saves him. On the day when the child knows for himself that God alone is the foundation for his life, when like the child Samuel he hears his name called and answers, " Speak, for thy servant hears " (I Sam. 3:10), then he is ready to become a full member of the Christian community. He "confirms" the baptismal vows made for him in infancy by his parents.[10]

The church teaches through the participation of families in the worshiping community. The place of the family in the church is receiving increasing attention today, and much research has gone into recent books on the subject. Part of the concern has been to find techniques by which to integrate families into the activity of the church. Here the thought is to ask how the family as a living group participating in the life of the church is a part of the teaching of the church.

There is a twofold action within the relationship between families and the church: the witnessing action of the family through corporate worship, and the action of the Holy Spirit in the life of the family which stems from that worship. A classic treatise on the relationship of church and home was written by Horace Bushnell in 1847. He recognized an organic unity between family life in the church and the covenanted families of Israel. The family participates in the life in Christ, receiving its own deepest life from this source by the Holy Spirit. Bushnell wrote:

"Probably enough there may be some of you that, without being Christians yourselves, are yet careful to teach your children all the saving truths of religion. . . . But how poor a teacher of Christ is anyone who is not in the light of Christ, and does not know the inward power of his truth as a gospel of life to the soul." [11]

The family, worshiping together within the church, bears witness to God's activity in creating and sustaining that family and in redeeming family relationships day by day. The child who participates with his family becomes aware of how these relationships interact. This is not a question as to the age at which a child should attend divine worship or the length of time that he should stay when he goes. The concern here is to note that when a family worships together this may be a channel for the grace of God to be operative within that group of people. The presence of children is so unusual in many churches today that a parent is often startled when a child prefers worshiping with his family to attending a church school class. Middle-class American culture has tended to segregate parents and children, and there are few times when a family participates together anywhere. Through such family action the church acknowledges that redemption begins at birth and families are given power, by the Holy Spirit, to love one another with that love which is from God.

AN UNDERSTANDING OF TEACHING

Some teaching is done by particular members whom the church chooses. Individuals within the community teach, and in so doing they represent the church and speak in behalf of the church. The teacher finds that certain conclusions follow from the representative nature of his task. He is not free to teach his private opinions, but mediates the ongoing experience of Christian faith, seen through the norm of the *kērygma*. This limitation is not meant as a deliberate bondage of the teacher, for presumably the church chooses as teachers for the young those whose lives are already a witness to God's redeeming love. The teacher will hope that the child too may share this experience, responding to God's grace and freely committing himself to the Christian life. The teacher represents the church in the remembered past and in present activity. He is given the task of making this past relevant as the child is related to the living Christ. In representing the church, the living body of Christ, the teacher bears a high responsibility.

The teacher is able to accept this responsibility as he is himself committed to the gospel. His teaching becomes a form of witness, and witness is a work of the Holy Spirit through the believer. Only Christians, by the grace of God, can make other Christians.

One can only teach as one comprehends. Regardless of the written material given for his guidance, a teacher reflects his own understandings in his relationships with a class. Even if he had only one written source for teaching, the Bible, he would necessarily mediate it to the children in terms of its meanings for himself. If he looked at it as a record of cultural history, he would so present it to his children. If he believed it to be the verbally inspired Word of God, he would in all sincerity teach it as such. If it is seen by him as the record of God's redemptive activity in history, that is how the children will see it through him. The orientation of a teacher's life and the presuppositions arising therefrom are important elements in teaching.

The teacher is an agent, mediating the gospel. This task cannot be accomplished by coercion, but only by love. Froebel and Pestalozzi embodied such understanding for those who watched them. Education often has been different for children since that day. Although the teacher cannot know the final result, he can be sure that his own involvement is a factor in that result. That is why the Christian community needs as teachers those who have themselves experienced the newness of life that God gives through Jesus Christ, and are committed to the *kērygma*. Such teachers can truly represent the church. They recognize that they are mediators through whom, in his own time and in his own way, God can speak in the hearts and lives of children. Having been made aware of the fullness of God's love in the cross and the resurrection, they are enabled to teach in love. They know the child as a " thou " who resists any attempt to force knowledge upon him, but who may respond freely to the personal disclosure given without thought of " successful " results.

The reason for teaching lies in this realization: that the church (and the individual on behalf of the church) is sent and therefore teaches. An amazing fact about the gospel is that those who have felt its power feel impelled to proclaim it. They have no choice, and yet they feel no bondage. They are glad witnesses to what God has done and is doing for them. The church knows itself to be God's creation through which Christ is made present in the world for each succeeding generation. The command in Matthew's Gospel, " Go therefore and make disciples of all nations " (Matt. 28:19), has seemed to be the command of the living Lord to his church in every place and every century. There are other reasons people might give as to why the church teaches: The church has a priceless heritage with meaning for each generation; it has a way of life that could transform existence; it is a witness in the world to the living God and to his Christ. All these are good and sufficient reasons, but they are by-products of the compelling reason. The church, thinking about its task, may find these reasons, but it knows that always, in back of these, there is a prior fact: namely, that God has sent it to proclaim the gospel and it cannot do otherwise.

The church conveys what it teaches. The past becomes part of the present and is an augur of the future. The church is itself a part of the teaching. Such teaching must not be made propositional. The Holy Spirit is the teacher and indwells the church. This fact makes it understandable why the church must convey what it teaches in a dynamic manner.

For these reasons the church cannot expect to be able to evaluate the results of its work by any yardstick that measures with precision. " I [Paul] planted, Apollos watered, but God gave the growth." (I Cor. 3:6.) This word from the apostle may well be taken to heart by the church whenever it is tempted to think of " success " in human terms. As Elmer G. Homrighausen puts it,

"Only God can make a Christian." [12] As the church carries out
its commission, God honors it with his redeeming work. The
personal response to God in Christ and growth in the Christian
life are events that have an inexplicable quality. They can neither
be foreseen nor planned, and when they happen they are accepted
as the gracious gift of the loving God.

It is said that when Adoniram Judson died, he left two converts
in all Burma. No twentieth-century missions board could have
afforded to keep that station on the books for so many years! But
today, a century and a half later, Burma has a higher percentage
of Christians in the population than has any other country in
Asia. "Unless a grain of wheat falls into the earth and dies . . ."
(John 12:24.) The redeemed life is a gift of God, and no person,
or even the Christian community, can take credit for the expression of the love of God new-found in another's life. To be able
so to witness that others may be added to the community is its
own reward.

The church does not exist to save the world, but to keep alive
by remembrance the holy work of God. The church has an immediate task which God has given. Because it is a very part of
the gospel, its existence brings to remembrance God's saving activity in the event of Jesus Christ. As the church fulfills this responsibility, God will use its witness in the saving of the world.
God sent his Son into the world that the world through him
might be saved — and the church is his body today. But when
and how the world will be saved is in God's keeping. Doubtless
he understands the ardor for his work which makes certain
among his people affirm that they will save the world in their
generation, but the parable of the wheat and the tares is a reminder of the realism in the Biblical view of redemption. That
the reign of God may come so that his will is done on earth as
in heaven is the prayer of the church, but the final fulfillment of
prayer always rests with God.

This understanding of the nature of the church's task relieves
much of the stress and strain in the world. There is no need to
push almost beyond endurance in one's own strength; there is no

need for intense competition, for anxious looking toward the resurgence of pagan faiths or the falling away of Christians in a particular part of the world. Wherever and whenever the church, by its life and work, witnesses to God's redeeming love by proclaiming the *kērygma*, God's purposes for the world are being fulfilled in it and through it, and it is being true to the Great Commission.

The content of the church's teaching is found in the basic message of the early church, the *kērygma*, and the resultant forms of teaching, the *didachē*. That could be simply another contribution to historicism, a new way of dissecting old manuscripts, or a different insight into what the first Christians thought.

Such has not been the result. It might be conjectured that the theological questions raised in Europe in the 1920's sent the scholars back to the Biblical records with different needs from those which had faced earlier seekers. The new needs were met through form-criticism and an understanding of the Bible as the record of "saving history." The proclamation is not a historic relic, but an integral part of the life of the church, as relevant today as when it was first proclaimed.

New Testament thought may at first glance seem alien to the contemporary mind. The result could be a tendency to avoid facing the fact of the *kērygma* by confining it to the faraway and long ago. However, the seeming archaism may not be the real reason, for any position becomes contemporary when it is accepted. Moreover, the gospel seemed strange in the first century and many rejected it because of its radical challenge. The distinction in viewing the gospel is not a matter of the century in which one lives, but of the contrast between the old age and the new. The proclamation arises from the event of Jesus Christ, which transforms life. The power of the redemption wrought through Jesus is available for all times — the new age has already begun. This is not proposition, but power. That is why one cannot set forth the *kērygma* in strictly conceptual terms. Christian education stands ready to receive such a message. Having accepted from pragmatic experimentalism a bent toward freer forms in materials and methods, it quite naturally set itself against any revival of theology in propositional terms. This opposition during the decade from 1935 to 1945, while American theologians were reformulating their own insights in reaction to nineteenth-century liberalism, has conserved the dynamic quality of its methodology to use with this Biblical expression of theology.

That the leaders in Christian education share the faith of the church as understood throughout the ecumenical world today, is to be seen in this quotation from the restudy report of the International Council of Religious Education, now the Division of Christian Education of the National Council of the Churches of Christ in the U.S.A.:

> " The focus of Christian revelation is found in Jesus Christ. He is the embodiment of the gospel, the good news of the saving grace and power of God. In him God was reconciling the world to himself. God commended his love toward us in the death of his Son. Here was more than man's utmost devotion to the divine will. Here was the redemptive act of God himself through a human life in history." [13]

The teaching, *didachē*, is derived from the *kērygma,* as we have seen. This needs to be stressed today because of the preponderance of moralism in current church school curriculum. *Kērygma* precedes *didachē,* but the latter cannot be absent from any full-rounded understanding of the Christian faith. The failure of the church has been in stressing *didachē* alone, as though God made demands upon persons but helped them only when they showed signs of failing. Examples are given: a child must learn to walk alone; an adolescent must have experience in making decisions. This is one way of looking at life, but contemporary scholars do not see that as the primary emphasis in the Gospels. Nevertheless, the kerygmatic account in Mark's Gospel is in the same company with the teaching materials known as the Sermon on the Mount, and both have had continuing relevance for the Christian life.

One may not avoid the fact that Pelagian-Arminian ideas have had their place and a corrective value in Christian thought. The

letter to the Romans with its emphasis on salvation by faith, and
the homily of James, "So faith by itself, if it has no works, is
dead" (James 2:17), do not cancel out each other. But whenever
a generation seeks God's favor primarily by works, the ringing
cry of the Reformation, "Faith alone!" (*sola fidei*), breaks into
efforts at upholding human sufficiency.

The existence of the church witnesses to what God has done
and is doing, i.e., its existence witnesses to the *kērygma*. This is
the distinctive message which the church carries. Ethical teaching
can be duplicated in other religions and in philosophy. The dynamic in back of the Christian teaching is the unique insight of
Christian faith. When that is understood, there is no talk of a
time when the church shall be the leaven that puts a new spirit
into the world, losing its identity in the process. The church is a
personal "thou" as the individual is a personal "thou," and is
called into existence by the personal God who has commissioned
it. The only way whereby it would lose its life would be through
faithlessness to its divine call, by losing the sense of a unique
mission and becoming a part of the world. Then God could no
longer use it (although he would not forsake it; that is his
covenantal promise).

The church exists to declare and not to command. John A.
Mackay has seen this as the distinction between the indicative
mood and the imperative mood. He says:

> "It cannot be too much emphasized that a great indicative,
> something that God has done, and not a great imperative,
> something that man should do, is the primary element in the
> Christian religion. The divine imperative is founded upon a
> redemptive act enshrined in a divine indicative." [14]

It should be understood that in basing the existence of the
church on the *kērygma* and seeming to place that before the
didachē, no evaluational priority is intended. People are human
and not divine, and although they may live by the Holy Spirit
they still need the assurance the ethical teaching gives. The priority is rather one of time. Because the church has been given the

kērygma, it follows that there can be Christians who are able to find help in the *didachē*.

The content of the *didachē* is related to saving events in personal history. This " personal history" is historical as well as present, and is a part of God's continuing activity. Establishing this relatedness in teaching, however, is a problem that is still to be faced in the field of Christian education. Teaching as instruction does not necessarily lead to faith, whether this teaching be understood as the mediation of doctrine or the clarification of the Scriptures. The method of the early church, as of the mission field today, was to proclaim the gospel as the way to faith; teaching as instruction came later to strengthen faith and to deepen the knowledge of faith.

The work of the Christian teacher is both to lead and to guide. Because he is more mature in the faith, the child looks toward him, accepting his ways and his words. This is why the teacher needs to sense that he is a channel for the Holy Spirit's making himself known to the learner. For the leader may be tempted to think of himself and his ways as the ultimate in learning, but the guide knows that he is leading beyond himself to a fulfillment envisaged, but not yet attained.

Here again is the difference between imposing knowledge on persons as objects and bringing about a relationship between personal subjects. It faces the curriculum writer. The presses are filled with " how to " books, attractively printed, journalistically interesting, imparting instructions in a nutshell. "If only one could write like that for church school teachers! " is the longing of editors and writers. But it cannot be so. Christian nurture is dynamic, and the gospel will not be reduced to a set of five steps. New methods of teaching grow out of new understandings of the task and the message, but they will not necessarily be simple to write or to use. The attempt to teach in logical progression threatens to destroy the vitality of the teaching for those who are thus nurtured.

The " what " conditions the " how." Methods are media, merely means for accomplishing an end. It is always possible, in complete sincerity, to use wrong means toward a right end. That is why methodology is in constant process of re-evaluation. Emil Brunner has a word on that subject. He writes:

> "We are certainly not concerned here with a question of 'mere psychology.' *What* I should say to a man upon his death-bed is a holy matter; but it is a matter no less holy how I am to say it to him in such a way that he shall understand and appreciate it. A pastor might — to put it somewhat strongly — go to heaven on account of the What but go to hell on account of the How. To despise the question of the How is a sign, not of theological seriousness, but of theological intellectualism. The What is, as it were, guarded by faith, but the How has to be guarded by love. But where the How and therefore love is lacking, there faith must be lacking also." [15]

Methodology is important. That "what" of Christian nurture is so to make known the *kērygma* that growing children may respond to God's saving love made known in Christ and live in relationship to him, committing their lives to him and finding the gift of the Holy Spirit through the life of the church to empower them in their every relationship. The "how" for this accomplishment is still to be explored.

6

Life-centered Methods: Participation

THE MEANING OF THE TERM

Methods for Christian teaching should be life-centered. The term
" life-centered " has been used ever since pragmatism became a
regnant philosophy for education. It usually has meant " experience-centered," and this reference has connoted present experience. The result was an intense interest in the moment and clear
plans for the future, but only a fragmentary view of the past,
which was construed as usable primarily in order to enrich the
present. Now the view of " life-centered " takes on a deeper connotation through the insights of the existentialist theologians and
philosophers. Existence, rather than abstract being, is deemed
important. Existence comprises a totality — not the self by itself,
but the self in relationship to others, things, the universe, and
history.

PARTICIPATION THROUGH HISTORIC EVENTS

Participation is a central factor in life-centered teaching, but
the meaning is deeper than that usually understood in education.
It means not only personal participation in a present group situation, although that is its most obvious meaning. Such participation can be encouraged through techniques that have been developed in recent years. There is a further level in participation in
which the self apprehends the persons with whom he participates;
and beyond that there is the ability to participate with persons
in historic events.

This is paralleled in cultural education by the recent stress on the teaching of history. Within the pragmatic framework, history is " put in its place." The teacher is careful to reconstruct the past as the past. Sometimes it is deliberately modernized — a technique occasionally used for the staging of classical dramas. With such methods, history is separated from the present by a wide gap. A parallel in the church school might be seen in units on " shepherd life in Palestine " or " the world in which Jesus lived." The modernizing method is used in constructing a drama about a present-day good Samaritan, or in producing a narrative such as that of the long-time best seller *In His Steps*.

To make historic acts real and to bridge the gap of the centuries so that the person is aware of his immediate situation while participating in past events — that is an existential approach, and it will require its own techniques. In the church such teaching will come by participation with those historic events and persons that have borne the proclamation of the gospel. One can speculate *about* ideas; one tends to be drawn *into* events. The Bible is primarily a record of events. The young Christian participates with Paul, carrying the gospel over land and sea, his whole life filled with the fullness of Christ. He lives with Peter, who denied his Lord but finally died for him; with Luther, who strove to accomplish the right; with Augustine, who tried many paths before his Lord found him.

This reflects back to the fact that when God wanted to teach mankind, he did so through the Word made flesh. The spoken word and the action in event were climaxed by word and action in a particular Person. God still teaches who he is and what he does through that Person. Irenaeus, indeed, carried the point farther when he described Jesus as recapitulating the experience of the race in his life. Irenaeus pressed the point needlessly through the events of the Old Testament, but he made it clear that Jesus was at all points human. Yet whereas all men from the beginning of time sinned and fell short of loving obedience to God, Jesus alone fulfilled that perfect obedience of the Son to the Father, thereby breaking the power of evil, sin, and death.

The new age had dawned and new life had come to earth. This happened once, but it happened for all time.

When the learner sees himself as he is, with all his needs and hopes, he identifies with those who knew the Lord in the flesh: with friendly Andrew, ambitious John, and doubting Thomas; and he knows that human persons and human needs are bridged. The gap of the centuries is closed.

This is not a completely imaginative type of learning, as in the reading of fiction, for He of whom one learns is made present to the believer. There is participation in events connected with God's redeeming work. Events and persons speak to persons as ideas cannot. Many people do not think conceptually, but all people understand happenings; hence the power of a good story or a vivid film scenario.

Persons learn how to teach as they recall the way by which they are taught by God. In the Biblical view, his teaching came through events of deliverance and wrath. The arrogant young Joseph came out of the pit a different person, and in Egypt found not only personal deliverance but deliverance for his people. He said to his brothers, " It was not you who sent me here, but God " (Gen. 45:8). The Book of Judges is a repeated record of oppression (wrath), repentance, and deliverance.

" And the Ammonites crossed the Jordan to fight also against Judah and against Benjamin and against the house of Ephraim; so that Israel was sorely distressed.

" And the people of Israel cried to the Lord, saying, ' We have sinned against thee, because we have forsaken our God and have served the Baals.' And the Lord said to the people of Israel, ' Did I not deliver you from the Egyptians and from the Amorites, from the Ammonites and from the Philistines? . . . Yet you have forsaken me and served other gods; therefore I will deliver you no more. Go and cry to the gods whom you have chosen; let them deliver you in the time of your distress.' And the people of Israel said to the Lord, ' We have sinned; do to us whatever seems good to thee; only deliver us, we pray thee, this day.' So they put away the foreign gods from among them and served the Lord; and he became indignant over the misery of Israel." (Judg. 10:9-16.)

This is the story that continues throughout the record of the Kingdoms of Israel and Judah. It is in the word of the Lord to the prophet concerning the invader from the East, "Assyria, the rod of my anger" (Isa. 10:5); and later of Cyrus, the invader from Persia, "I gird you, though you do not know me" (Isa. 45:5). As the wrath of God had delivered his people to Nebuchadnezzar, so his saving work raised up Cyrus the Persian to make possible their return from exile. Judas did not repent, but fled from the Lord he helped to crucify, and destroyed himself. Peter faced his risen Lord, was forgiven, and received the commission, "Feed my lambs" (John 21:15). This is saving history: when man turns aside from God he sins; but when he repents, God in his loving mercy restores him.

God teaches through events. To the "objective" observer, the nonparticipant, these events are not held together in a meaningful relation. He says, "I would not cause such persons to suffer; either God is wicked or he does not exist." The "involved" persons know otherwise. He who sees with eyes of faith, and trusts God beyond the turn of the road, knows that "in everything God works for good with those who love him, who are called according to his purpose" (Rom. 8:28). Paul wrote those words after he already had suffered for the Lord. He continued with the assurance that nothing in all creation could separate us from the love of God in Christ Jesus our Lord.

A psalmist, centuries earlier, had written, "Surely the wrath of men shall praise thee" (Ps. 76:10). Another writer of hymns, centuries later, was to write:

> "When through the deep waters I call thee to go,
> The rivers of woe shall not thee overflow;
> For I will be with thee thy troubles to bless,
> And sanctify to thee thy deepest distress."

When a teacher grasps this understanding that God shows his love and brings his children unto himself through personal suffering and tragic events, there will be no need for extra lesson materials trying to explain why there are earthquakes, floods, and fires, or why people sometimes die young. "Nature" does not give answers, but only analogies and rationalizations. The Biblical witnesses may say quite frankly, "We do not know; we only know that God sustains us and fulfills his purposes through all events." Existential participation in the redeeming events of the Bible helps to bring such an awareness.

REMEMBRANCE, A FACTOR IN PARTICIPATION

Remembrance is an important function and a distinctively human one. This has not been too well recognized by recent educational writers of the experimentalist school who have considered reasoning to be the distinctively human activity. Since the psychological work of Sigmund Freud, however, there is a need to take seriously the place of remembrance in the life of persons and groups. Remembrance makes maturation possible, for it gives man a sense of time. He knows what the past is, and the older he grows the longer is his remembering. To the little child, "yesterday" is all past time. The older child, like the adult, knows yesterday both as time and as duration. He also knows whether it seems a long time ago or a short time ago, and that depends on the pleasure the intervening hours brought.

Remembrance makes love possible, and the deepening of love across the years. Love does not increase simply by the progression of time, but by the remembrance of the events of the intervening years since love first began. Indeed, love does not so much increase, as going from less to more, but rather it multiplies, being great even from the beginning. Karl Barth's phrase to the effect that man is a man and not a cat is apropos here, because while the cat enjoys receiving affection, he has too short a memory to know of its continuance.

Because memory brings time and love, it also makes possible both the duration and intensity of suffering. The duration is bound up with time and the intensity with love. This too is involved in the "why" questions which children ask and which the Sunday church school lessons have vainly tried to answer in terms of the healing sunshine and the ever-returning spring. Time, love, and suffering are not cyclic; they are ongoing. Death too is bound up in all these. The cat who has lost her kitten seems to have forgotten within a few hours, or a few days. Not so the mother who has lost a child.

Remembrance also can bring the distant close, whether it be of time or of space. One says. " It seemed as if it were yesterday," or " He seemed so close; one could hardly believe he was a thousand miles away." This is the aspect of remembrance that makes the historical event contemporaneous. In something of this manner the Christian community remembers the past.

The Bible is best understood in this context of remembrance. Remembrance alone does not give meaning, but it keeps the record alive until meaning is given. The early community preserved authentic records of the life of Jesus because they faithfully related their memories of him even when they did not fully understand the meaning of events. Only as God illumines events do they take on redemptive meaning.

God, through his revealing activity, also helps the person or the community to remember what has been forgotten. Here is an insight that has come from psychoanalysis: that persons tend to forget what they wish to forget, or what they cannot face. In Christian understanding, God brings the buried past into consciousness and makes it possible for the person to face it and learn from it, whether the event be in personal history or in the history of the community. The adaptation of the gospel to each century may not be entirely on the basis of a present need, but may also include a present wish to forget. The pedagogical purpose of remembrance is to heal and to make whole — to provide a channel for the saving work of God.

The Bible seen as remembrance has a relevance which is difficult to find when one tries too insistently to put the reader into the original setting. This realization helps the curriculum writer to look anew at the way he retells the Biblical record to children. The very frame of reference may be a forgetting rather than a remembering. It may be well to identify with the boy who brought his lunch to Jesus, but to admire the generosity of his act rather than the wonder of what God was able to do through him is to forget and distort the point of view of the original writer. To tell a story of Jesus' appreciation of the birds and flowers is to forget what Jesus himself could never have forgotten in the light of the two thousand years of remembered history given to him in his own childhood: that Israel did not worship nature, but God the Creator and Savior, known through the historical life of his people. Perhaps it was this feeling for remembrance within the church that made it continually tell children of how Jesus called the little ones to himself.

Such a view prevents the writer and teacher from burying the Bible in history. It explains why the Biblical myths are not just like other myths for the Christian, the involved person. Both may be explanations for the same human phenomena, but the Biblical myths are set in the context of God's activity and they are a part of the Christian's own remembered past. Biblical history is also a part of his own history, explaining to him how God continuously has shown his loving care toward those whom he has called.

Hope is born of remembrance in the existential context of despair. There is no easy optimism today, even in the United States of America. As citizens, people are aware of the terrible responsibility they bear in the world; as individuals and as members of families, they are fearful for their very lives. The child apprehends something of the concern of the adults among whom he lives, but over and beyond this, he often has the feeling of being misunderstood, indeed, of not even understanding himself.

When the present moment is seen in the context of history, hope then arises. Hope does not spring from nothingness. Nothingness issues in nihilism, as the writings of Jean-Paul Sartre remind us. Hope springs from the remembrance of the past. It does not spring from a natural past, as children are so often taught when at Easter time the teacher says to them that each year God causes the seemingly lifeless flowers to bloom again.

Hope springs from the remembrance of the steadfast love of the Lord throughout history. This is why the affirmation of the psalmist speaks to each person who repeats it in the hour of need: "Surely goodness and mercy shall follow me all the days of my life" (Ps. 23:6). A dramatic example is found in Ps. 136, in which the writer recounts the mighty acts of God in creation, the deliverance from Egypt, and his care over his people in Israel. After each line runs the refrain "for his steadfast love endures for ever" (KJV, "mercy"). Here is the present activity of God seen continuously in the light of what he has always done for his people. Another illustration of the linking of assurance with the historical activity of God is to be found in John, ch. 6. Jesus has fed the multitude, and the people remind him that their fathers ate the manna in the wilderness. Jesus replies that it was God and not Moses who sent the bread from heaven. Then he says, "I am the bread of life; he who comes to me shall not hunger, and he who believes in me shall never thirst." (John 6:35.) This word was retold in the Christian community a generation after the event, yet it was known as a present word and not only as a past utterance; and so it continues to this day.

Hope is determined by the saving event. For Judaism, this has been the deliverance from Egypt. In the Psalms and by the prophets God's redemption of his people had been set in this context. "Come and see what God has done: he is terrible in his deeds among men. He turned the sea into dry land; men passed through the river on foot." (Ps. 66:5-6.) When Hosea appeals to Israel to forsake their adulterous ways and return to the God who loves them, the Word of the Lord recalls, "When Israel was a child, I loved him, and out of Egypt I called my son" (Hos. 11:1); he adds, "The more I called them, the more they went from me" (v. 2). There is no tenderer description anywhere in the Old Testament of the love of God than the words that follow:

> "Yet it was I who taught Ephraim to walk,
>   I took them up in my arms;
>   but they did not know that I healed them.
> I led them with cords of compassion,
>   with the bands of love." (Vs. 3-4.)

The saving event is always twofold: unless there had been bondage, there had been no need for deliverance. Therefore " Egypt " bears two meanings. The Word of the Lord continues, " They shall return to the land of Egypt, and Assyria shall be their king, because they have refused to return to me " (v. 5). The wrath of God is loving wrath — a term that those who have known the love of God can understand. The Word continues:

> " How can I give you up, O Ephraim!
> How can I hand you over, O Israel! . . .
> My heart recoils within me,
> my compassion grows warm and tender." (V. 8.)

The event that was so vivid when Hosea wrote in the eighth century B.C. is equally vivid today, when, on the Friday evening of the first full moon after the vernal equinox, Jewish families gather in their homes to re-enact the event, assured that now as then, in the United States of America, in Germany, or in Israel, they are children of the covenant, and God will never forsake his own.

The central saving events for the Christian community are the crucifixion and resurrection of Jesus Christ the Lord. The largest portion of each of the Gospel records is the Passion narrative, a well-developed record rather than a series of fragmentary remembrances as are the earlier parts of the Gospels. Here is the *kērygma* as found in the apostolic preaching. " They put him to death by hanging him on a tree; but God raised him on the third day and made him manifest; not to all the people but to us who were chosen by God as witnesses, who ate and drank with him after he rose from the dead." (Acts 10:39-41.) Paul records it in his letters, carefully noting that this is not his own thinking, but consists of words given to him: " For I delivered to you as of first importance what I also received, that Christ died for our sins in accordance with the scriptures, that he was buried, that he was raised on the third day in accordance with the scriptures, and that he appeared to Cephas, then to the twelve " (I Cor. 15:3-5). It is echoed in The First Letter of Peter: " Come to him, to that living stone, rejected by men but in God's sight chosen and precious" (I Peter 2:4). And in The Letter to the Hebrews: "When Christ had offered for all time a single sacrifice for sins, he sat down at the right hand of God." (Heb. 10:12.)

Each year the Christian community remembers that God sent his Son into the world, that by his suffering and death men might become aware of the meaning of sin; to turn and repent, and be reconciled to God, and so to be enabled to share in the resurrection event; to know Christ, not only crucified but also risen.

This remembrance is made known not only on the yearly event of Easter, but also in the personal, once-in-a-lifetime event of baptism. For baptism, as has been pointed out, is a participation in the dying and rising of Christ the Lord.

The saving act of God in Christ is further brought to remembrance through the Lord's Supper, celebrated daily in some parts of the church, weekly among some other Christian bodies, and less frequently among still others. Here is Christ the Lord present among his people; they participate in the body of Christ. They are made one with him and with one another. Here in truth are past, present, and future known in one single moment and event. For the minister or priest, standing before a congregation, holds before them the bread, saying, "Take, eat; this is my body, which is broken for you," and addresses them further, "This do in remembrance of me. . . . For as often as ye eat this bread, and drink this cup, ye do show the Lord's death till he come." Nothing else in Christian experience equals the totality of existential participation that is apprehended in the action of the believer in receiving the Holy Communion.

The Christian year is also a way of remembrance as the life of the Lord is re-enacted from season to season within the community of the church. Indeed, for the individual Christian, life has often been seen as a *daily* dying and rising with the Lord. As manna was given day by day, so is the grace of God imparted in each moment, for each event. The Christian life is dynamic. In sin one dies, and by repentance one is raised into newness of life through the Holy Spirit. In this, as in the physical needs of life, comes the word: "Do not be anxious about tomorrow, for tomorrow will be anxious for itself. Let the day's own trouble be sufficient for the day" (Matt. 6:34). When Paul prayed that his affliction be removed, the Lord answered, "My grace is sufficient for you, for my power is made perfect in weakness" (II Cor. 12:9).

A life-centered teaching begins with participation in the historic events which are made present by remembrance.

A CHILD'S PARTICIPATION THROUGH PRESENT EXPERIENCE

The child's needs, tasks, and capacities are being subjected to new research today, and no final words are being spoken. The approach, however, is dynamic; the child's growth is seen in terms of the whole person (organismic). Particular attention is being paid to the role of emotions in the interaction of the whole life. Development is understood as being continuous, purposive, and involving the whole person. Moreover, it is observed that where the needs and tasks are not met as they arise, the task of growth is made more difficult both for the person involved and for other persons in the family.

A child is understood to have certain basic needs. The concern of the church in teaching is mainly with the needs of the self and of the self in relationship to others. The basic need is for security as known through affection. Without this, failure in many areas may result; with it, a child can endure a remarkable degree of hardship. After security he needs status, a sense of belonging, and the approval both of those in authority over him and of his peers.

A child has also some specific needs as he grows: increasing self-direction, a balance between success and failure, a growing harmony with reality, progressive symbolization, and the attainment of individuality. Along with these needs, a child has certain developmental tasks to fulfill as he grows. Some of these are non-recurrent (such as learning to walk and to talk). Others recur over a lifetime (such as getting along with people, or learning to distinguish right from wrong). The life situations through which a child grows are as many and as varied as the child and environment can produce by interaction in home and community, church and school, at work or at play. Such understandings of the child's needs, tasks, and life situations have caused a re-evaluation of the idea of "readiness" and the introduction of the word "timeliness." While readiness involves interest and need, timeliness involves deeper personality factors reflecting emotional needs and developmental tasks. Whether or not a child has the capacity to face each task and life situation as it arises will depend in part on the extent to which his basic needs are being met. For this reason it is important for parents and teachers to try to see the child as he sees himself rather than to strive for an objective point of view as to his needs.

The child has certain capacities as a member of the human race, some of which are more pertinent to a discussion of Christian nurture than are others equally important in his growth. Some of his potentialities are part of his individual personality. His growth from day to day and from year to year is a result of the interaction of his total self with other persons and the physical environment in a whole pattern. In the normal course of events his capacities are sufficient for his tasks; thus at a given stage of development, he both needs to talk in order to express his emotions, and has the physical capacity to form words. Every "normal" child is able to give and to receive love, to live in companionship with other people, to think, and to imagine. But each particular child's level of achievement, in these as in specific learnings, will vary in accordance with the configuration of his life.

The task of Christian nurture is to put his present experience in a context that will give him something to remember. He will remember that which has relevance, and will participate in those events and persons in the past history of the church which will help and sustain him.

When he can see his needs and problems against those of Biblical persons, he has a focus beyond himself from which to view himself. The story of Joseph and his brothers, which we mentioned above, is an example. Joseph, the next-to-the-youngest child and his father's favorite, was hardly in a position to be liked by the rest. He sought status by reporting dreams in which he was the center of the universe. The result was his utter rejection: he was driven from his home and put into the pit. It was not until Joseph was in Egypt that the saving word came: " The Lord was with Joseph " (Gen. 39:2).

Now this is not to suggest the psychologizing of Bible stories, but only to indicate that they show a penetrating understanding of the dynamics of human need and response. The hero story of David and Goliath was told to all small children until a generation arose who discovered in college that Elhanan and not David may have been the hero. After this discovery, parents and teachers hesitated, in their disillusionment, to relate it further. Yet the tale has profound insight. When Saul says, " You are not able to go against this Philistine to fight with him; for you are but a youth," David replies, " The Lord who delivered me from the paw of the lion and from the paw of the bear, will deliver me from the hand of this Philistine." (I Sam. 17:33, 37.) A child sensing his own feelings of " lostness " will respond to the story of the search for Jesus in the Temple by Mary and Joseph, and will feel wonder before their child, who felt secure because he was in his Heavenly Father's house. The jealousies and strivings for status are reflected in the disciples, who learned from their Lord that real status is known only to God. " Close grading " needs reinterpretation when the subject under consideration is the deeper needs of the self. Fear has the same feeling to the kindergarten child as it has for the adolescent; the need for affection is as strong in adulthood as it is in infancy. Neither age, intellectual ability, nor social maturity affects their ever-present reality. Teacher and pupils have a common bond. This viewpoint conceivably could open up a whole new way of thinking about the Biblical materials to be used with children at different ages. It is possible that adults have sentimentalized the child and not been fully aware of the depths of his existence.

A British mother has written with discernment of the spiritual growth of her two small children and of their relationships within the family. Writing under the thesis that "there is in children an unconscious knowledge of many truths which are described later in terms of theology," she proceeds:

> "The child who minds nothing more than being estranged, finds it impossible to remain in perfect harmony: his very development upsets relationships both within himself and between himself and the Other, and causes disharmony, estrangement, the sense of sin; and following on this the effort to make right by eliminating the bad, and the consequent fear of being eliminated (for he cannot wish to eliminate something or part of a person without feeling that he himself is in danger). But this brings a return of the feeling of denial of one's right to live (frustration) and causes further anger and thus further fear. So the need to be 'saved' from the impasse; the need for atonement and the experience of sacrifice with all that may lead to later in doctrines of redemption." [1]

The creeds, formulated by the ancient church, have given to generations the assurance that their basic needs *are* met: God is their Father, Christ is their Savior, guilt is removed and sin is forgiven the repentant, fellowship is offered in the church, the fear of death is overcome in the affirmation of eternal life.

Although one may begin with the existential situation of the child, this receives historical depth as it is seen in the context of other lives, which are made contemporary by the fact that they too have shared with us both in the need for and in the receiving of the saving grace of God.

This broader context deepens present experience. The learner is not alone. Others have felt this way. God who saved then can save now. The child is surrounded by the company of believers, the fellowship of those who have been called, the body of whom Christ is the head and which is indwelt by the Holy Spirit. Here are security and love. Here can be for them the witness to what God is still doing. A child's participation is involved in the participation of the adults who surround him.

THE TEACHER'S ROLE IN PARTICIPATION

The teacher is a guide as well as a fellow participant with the child. He has the same needs as the child, although these are expressed in different immediate yearnings. He too knows fears, needs friends, wants to accomplish something useful.

This fact should help him to understand the child. With understanding comes acceptance. The child is no "better" and no "worse" than the adults who work with him in the life of the church, although when teachers talk of discipline problems there is often a groping around to find a place to lay blame. The child who comes on Sunday morning should be able to expect an awareness of his needs and problems from those who meet him as Christian teachers. This is true if, as so often happens today, his daily schoolteacher is well versed in the art of understanding her pupils. It is true also, if, as sometimes happens, there has been too little understanding at home or at school.

In so far as he is conscious of his own need of God's redeeming grace, the teacher will be aware of his pupil's need. As he has known faith and rejoices in living the Christian life, he shares these things with the children through his very presence in a room with them, as they talk and act together once a week. He can understand failure and success, weakness and strength, for he too has met these and can remember them from his recent experience — and even from his own childhood. Such a teacher might begin a class session with " I remember when I was about nine years old, my mother told me to pick some papers which had been torn all over the living room floor. I hadn't done it — my little brother had. I thought it very unfair. Has anything like that ever happened to you? " Children will begin to recall incidents, and soon they will be facing the question: " How do we feel when this kind of thing happens? Why do brothers and sisters — and parents — act as they do? What is the best way for us to act — from everybody's standpoint? How does God help us to see what is best — and to do it? " Some verses from Ephesians — " Children, obey your parents in the Lord " and " Fathers, do not provoke your children to anger " (Eph. 6:1, 4) — will suggest: "What is the Bible saying? Does it throw any light on our questions?" The teacher, a parent perhaps as well as a former child, will become a participant in such a way as to help the children realize that adults too recognize the need for God's grace.

If the teacher's own remembered past is a help to him in participating in the Christian faith with his pupils, the remembrance of events and persons in the historic life of the Christian community — through the Bible and later events — will be a further enrichment and help for meeting their needs. The teacher can help the child so to participate with Biblical characters that these will become contemporary. They will emerge as if they were really living people, for they *were* real people. Biblical events will be made vivid and clear. The child will not find these by himself. The teacher will need to know what characters and situations can live for children. He will need the further skill to mediate that quality in story, conversation, or other methods. This means that he will want to increase his own knowledge of the contents of the Bible. He cannot rely on printed curriculum material alone, or even on the reading books that may supplement it. First, the Bible will need to become a living book for him; only as God has spoken to him through this Word, can he help the child to find God's word in it.

The teacher helps the child to see Biblical persons through their situation. Abraham was able to leave the familiar city of Ur and make his home elsewhere because he trusted God completely. (There are many "migrant" children today: not necessarily underprivileged, but children of the middle class who live in a different section of the country every few years while the fathers are climbing the ladder of success.) Children hearing ominous rumors at home of the dispersal of city dwellers before the threat of demolition bombing can understand the children of Palestine who left Jerusalem, weeping by the waters of Babylon, yet learning that no land was strange to God. Bible people become companions on the way. Historical remembrance comes to give the assurance that God still seeks and saves those who know themselves to be lost. The child in the present moment remembers that God loves him because persons in the Bible have witnessed to that fact.

This ability to make the Bible meaningful is part of the teacher's own experience as a Christian. He knows that the Christian life is one of witness. Then he is able to make these concrete actions and not mere words to be defined. He has found that the Christian life is one of demand, and yet one of satisfying fulfillment. Then he is able to show others that this is so. The guide is able to go before, because he knows the way.

Not every teacher has this faith, or has found this living word in the pages of the Bible. Yet it might happen through the teaching experience that a teacher becomes a participant who has not been so earlier. If he feels a hunger, God can fill him. Even before he realizes his needs, God is saving him through the Holy Spirit. Teaching is itself an opportunity to be taught of the one teacher, even Christ.

The teacher then becomes even more fully a participant along with the pupils. He reads the Bible to learn from its words and its events. As it speaks to him, he finds that which he can share with others, for their needs are also in his thoughts as he reads.

He participates in the class session through conversation and discussion. Children always think of the teacher as a person of another order from themselves. Even adults usually show a certain deference to the one designated as class leader, whatever the term used. This barrier can be broken down to the extent that the teacher is really a participant, acknowledging needs in himself similar to those in the persons he teaches. He hears their experiences and he shares his own. He is like them, and yet he is different. He can help them to see a fresh viewpoint: he speaks as parent or businessman or schoolteacher; he speaks of his interests and his hobbies.

Through such participation of teacher and class there comes a group-centered experience, a true form of learning. The teacher becomes a resource person, but one who himself has much to learn. Others may be better leaders of a particular discussion, formulators of questions, planners of the next steps. He takes the place where he is needed in the life of the group in order that he may best help each person. In so doing, he brings a new dimension to the teacher's role. It becomes just as important to be among the group as to be the " head " of the group. The sharing aspect of the Christian fellowship becomes understood through practical use. Each finds that his " place " is to give that which he can best give for the strengthening of others.

The teacher is a full participant in the life of the group because he, as much as any other member of the group, stands in need of the continuing grace of God. Every dedicated teacher soon notes with amazement that he is learning more than he can ever teach, and that he is growing in grace because of the responsibility he has accepted rather than through any adequately meritorious discharge of his responsibility.

The pupil participates through the teacher. The teacher is himself a medium for participation, but he is helped in his responsibility by the media of teaching that are at hand.

THE ARTS AS MEDIA FOR PARTICIPATION

The various arts are media for participation: painting, music, drama, poetry, and story, among others. These can bring the Biblical activity of God into present remembrance to meet the existential needs of the child within the Christian community. The great artist sees the depths of life and its wholeness. He has the genius to convey this understanding in a tangible form through which other people may participate in his insight. Great art is not simply factual; indeed, it need not be factual at all. The absence of " factuality " in many examples of great religious art may have occasioned the tendency in the pragmatic emphasis in Christian nurture to turn to the use of pictures, poetry, and music that seemed less artistic but more concrete. Thus there has been an emphasis on making sure that a Biblical picture has an authentic Palestinian background. What the faces of the depicted characters conveyed was less important. Objects, not subjects, were the matters under consideration. The *Last Supper* by a church school artist is therefore to be preferred over that of Leonardo da Vinci, because in ancient Palestine people did not sit on chairs at a table, but reclined at a low table.

This criterion for judging art in teaching is insufficient for a Christian nurture that seeks to convey the *kērygma*. The stress would be on the disclosure of God's activity as it is seen in the persons depicted, in the music, or in the words. Art would not always be Biblical, but it would be Biblically oriented. It might be a contemporary expression of the Biblical insight of God's saving work, although some of the finest present-day painting uses Biblical subjects as such, e.g., the Old Testament pictures of Chagall, and the paintings of the trial and crucifixion of Jesus by Rouault. There has been an objection to the use of classical art forms in religious education because they contained too much background. This could hardly be said of contemporary art, which tends to be starkly simple, using background only as a further illumination of the subject. Art tries to go beyond the outward appearance in order to convey inner meaning. This can be a rich medium for revealing the depths of the Christian faith and of expressing the *kērygma* with power.

Music is another art form through which the gospel can be communicated to the participant with power, whether he sings or listens. An excellent example is to be found in *The Passion According to St. John,* by Johann Sebastian Bach. The reading of the Gospel narratives in the services for Holy Week goes back to the fourth century. By the twelfth century this had become a dramatic musical liturgy. Bach brought to his composition the religious influences of the Protestant Reformation. The Gospel narrative is sung in recitative, interspersed by occasional simple chorales. Whether these were originally sung by the congregation or by the choir alone, the listeners tend to identify with this chorus, who express the feelings of the Christian viewing the awesome activity of God. When Jesus, confronted by the betrayer, says, "I am he; if ye seek for me, then let these go their way," the chorus responds, "Oh boundless love, Oh love beyond all telling . . . I live within the world, its pleasures cherish, and thou must perish! " When He is smitten in the court of the high priest, the chorus sings, "Who was it thus did smite thee? . . . 'Tis I by guilt encumbered." When Peter denies the Lord, the chorus prays, "Jesus, do thou look on me when I too forsake thee." [2]

Here is a kerygmatic approach to music. The gospel is proclaimed, and the listener is invited to respond. Chorales are simple; older children, studying the life of Jesus, could use the text for choric speaking, inserting several of the chorales that would have meaning for them.

Hymns have always been a source for the expression of Christian faith. The earliest hymns, those found in the New Testament, are all kerygmatic. So is "Shepherd of Tender Youth," one of the oldest hymns in our present hymnals, written by Clement of Alexandria, ca. 200. Much rethinking needs to be done on the subject of hymns for children so that simplicity is not stressed at the expense of imagination and moralization at the expense of response to God in Christ. Gregorian plainsong and Anglican chant are classic forms of church music, seldom used outside the liturgical churches for responsive purposes, although it is generally assumed that the Psalms were originally written to be sung.

Poetry is one of the subtler forms of expression, appearing obscure to a matter-of-fact age. Poets use imagery and symbolism in a form that children today have not been helped adequately to appreciate. The emphasis on the "here and now" has made much children's poetry little more than rhythmic prose. Christina Rossetti, in her poems for children, has caught basic Christian insights in a simple way. Christmas means to her not simply a baby born to parents in a strange place, but —

> "Love came down at Christmas,
>   Love all lovely, Love divine;
> Love was born at Christmas,
>   Star and angels gave the sign." [3]

"In the Bleak Midwinter" catches all the wonder of the incarnation. This ends with the well-known quatrain beginning,

" What can I give him? " Here is the note of personal participation characteristic of existential writing. The question raised in using the poem in the church school has been whether the phrase, " Give him my heart," would not literally puzzle the child. There also has been concern to separate in the child's mind the first two Persons of the Godhead, a procedure which has significant repercussions in later childhood.

Poetry is able to express the depths of emotions. Through it the reader can be aware of more than he completely understands. It leaves room for growth beyond the teacher's control, for the hearer must make its insights his own, according to his need and his ability to respond.

Drama is a vicarious experience, through which the person, whether he listens or takes part, is a participant. The mystery cycles of the late Middle Ages are examples of Biblical drama done in simple style which makes the action contemporaneous. The *Quem Quaeritis Trope* was written to be part of the Easter liturgy.[4] Modern Christian drama, as seen in the work of T. S. Eliot, for example, tends to be highly sophisticated and symbolic, although portions of *Murder in the Cathedral* have a forthright power, showing both the depths of Christian faith and the ambiguities within the personal response. Great drama seems beyond the apprehension of the child because of its complexity, but there remains a question as to how far drama should be diluted into playmaking in order that the medium of action may be used as a technique for teaching.

The elements of paradox and irony also enter into the consideration of the arts as media for participation. Pragmatic education has stressed synthesis, but existentialism insists that there are unresolvable factors in life which must exist side by side in order that life may have its true depth. Drama and poetry both stress this understanding, as does painting.

Storytelling is another of the arts, the one most used with children. Prose narrative has the capacity of conveying more understanding than do seemingly simple explanations of a situation. Adults and children alike are held by the power of a story that is well written or well told. The Old Testament is filled with such stories. To elaborate them is to dilute their impact, not, as is sometimes supposed, to clarify them. No retelling of the story of Jesus and the children is simpler than that contained in a few verses in the Gospel of Mark. There is need to see the story as an art form, rather than merely as a medium through which to give information or explain ideas. The great folk stories which the reading parent enjoys as much as the listening child — stories like "The Gingerbread Boy" or that modern classic, "Peter Rabbit" — have no counterpart in the customary retelling of the *kē-rygma*. Rhythm, repetition, accumulated excitement to a real climax, and a swift denouement — these are virtually unknown either in curriculum materials or books of Biblical stories.

Great art of any type is the fulfillment of the artist's vocation within the Christian community. The artist has been called of God to this task, just as the teacher is called to teach. The artist has a particular God-given talent. This is seen, for example, in the life of Johann Sebastian Bach, for many years organist at St. Thomas' Church, Leipzig. His devotion shone forth in the music through which the gospel was proclaimed, and it was affirmed in every page of manuscript, inscribed to the glory of God.

In using the insights of great artists through the centuries, the child and the teacher are linked by remembrance with the Christian communities of the several historical periods in their witness to what God does. There is a sense in which great art is not a "thing," because something of a person has gone into the making. Art cannot fully be understood apart from the artist and those factors in his life which elicited this expression of his existence. When children learn the Christmas chorale "From Heaven High," they are linked with Martin Luther's little boy and his companions, for whose Christmas pageant the great Reformer wrote the hymn.

This is the point at which to speak of the word "creative," which is used so frequently with reference to art forms today. Denis de Rougemont deals with the subject in an essay on "Religion and the Mission of the Artist." He writes:

"The use of the verb 'to create' in relation to human activity is, I believe, rather recent. This manner of speaking of the human act, by comparing it, or even equaling it, to the divine act, not only comes from a synergist doctrine which demands examination, but coincides historically with the impoverishment or loss in the modern epoch of the belief in a Creator God. I am not at all sure that man is capable of creating, in the true sense of this term: that is, of producing an absolute mutation, an absolute novelty in the universe. That which is currently called today a 'creation' is in reality only a slightly different arrangement of elements already known according to laws known or knowable. Therefore it is a *composition*. Before Romanticism, we were content to say that a musician composed an opera, that a painter composed a picture. But today, we say that he 'creates' a symphony, that he 'creates' forms. No one can prove that a man creates something, because no one can know the totality of existent things with their structures and their rapports. We shall limit ourselves, therefore, to the classical term 'composition' when speaking of works of art." [5]

There is a different focus in the term "composition." To "create" would make man seem to be equal to God, whereas the power to create was thought of classically as a unique activity of God, the term "Creator" being used as a name for God, but never for man. This point of view is particularly thought-provoking in the context of general religious education, for "creative" activities and "creative" teaching and even "creative" learning have been terms expressive of the purposes as well as the ideals of many who have worked with children during this century.

The child's experience is deepened as he is enabled to see it in the broader context which art discloses. He participates with the artist, who also has participated in the past, both in the message that he remembers and in the forms and technique for composition that are the bases for his art. Each century produces art that is the expression of its existence, yet each builds on the forms that were given by previous centuries. This too is remembrance. But in Christian art, the form is used for the expression of a particu-

lar content: the gospel, the proclamation of God's saving work
for men through Jesus Christ.

This is a field for curriculum enrichment that has been virtually untouched. It will require both research to find materials
and experimentation to discover the child's response at different
ages. If Christian nurture is to be given the depth and breadth
which come from being linked with the continuing Christian
community and from recognizing the never-failing creative and
redemptive activity of God, this will be a task well worth under-
taking.

Life-centered Methods: Recognition and Communication

RECOGNITION AS ENCOUNTER

Participation is a form of learning open to even the smallest child. Recognition is an awareness that comes through participation, but which is a personal response on the part of the learner. It is a mood of reverence, for it is the point at which the person hears his name called by God and makes reply.

This has been called "encounter," the meeting of the I and Thou. It is the recognition of the personal God, who makes his presence known in history: the realization that in truth God is with men. The Bible offers many instances. Two persons on the road to Emmaus walked with the Lord but did not know him until he broke bread for them. Saul had heard of Jesus, but did not encounter him until the event on the Damascus road.

The place of encounter is being increasingly recognized as a factor in education. This may be described as the encounter between professor and student or between the student and the truth. It is related to the psychological term "insight." The understanding of developmental tasks and a fresh definition of "readiness" point in the direction of situations at which confrontation takes place.

The developmental tasks with religious significance are those concerned with the understanding of the self and of one's relationships with other persons, and the way through which the individual accepts the turning from one " stage " of life into the next.[1] In such crises of development God speaks to the person, offering to sustain and guide him so that he need have no fear. To face God and respond to him, accepting his love, is to walk with him.

There is a definite aloneness to this encounter, even though it may take place within a group and be prepared for by the surrounding fellowship of the church. God calls to all men, but the address is to each man personally and each must answer for himself. Education may lead people to Christ, but the Holy Spirit, in his own time, will make a person aware of the One in whose presence he stands. Moreover, this call does not presage a better adjustment to the standards of the surrounding environment, but may set the individual out of harmony with his group. This is the point at which the church is recognized as the fellowship of those who are called out.

To encounter God means to recognize him; it also means to cease avoiding him. To see God is to see the difference between God and oneself — for if God were not different from a human being, he could not be God. To know God's love is to be sorry for all separation from him, and true repentance brings reconciliation.

This is effected through prayer. Prayer is the attitude of reverent recognition through which the person encounters God. Chronological age and mental development give no clue as to the time of encounter. A six-year-old, lacking human love and affection, may be found of God and filled with his love. A twelve-year-old, being self-sufficient in every way, may never have heard his call.

The depth of a child's encounter is strengthened by participation with those of the past who have prayed. There is the child Samuel, who at an early age heard his name called by God and responded, receiving the word for adults who did not hear. One participates understandingly in the lives of earlier members of the Christian fellowship by praying in their words — by using prayers of Augustine, Luther, or Wesley, for example. The collects of *The Book of Common Prayer* are classical expressions of prayer through which the church today is linked in remembered participation with the church across the centuries, and is given treasured words through which to express the recognition of God's purposes. When the literal meaning of " prevent " is explained, here is one of the simplest of collects: " Lord, we pray thee that thy grace may always prevent and follow us, and make us continually to be given to all good works; through Jesus Christ our Lord. Amen." This collect for the Seventeenth Sunday after Trinity recognizes the priority of God's activity to man's ability to show his faith in daily living. The collect for the Second Sunday after Christmas Day, using the imagery of the Fourth Gospel, has the same thought in vivid language: " Almighty God, who hast poured upon us the new light of thine incarnate Word; grant that the same light enkindled in our hearts may shine forth in our lives; through Jesus Christ our Lord. Amen."

Encounter also comes through worship, which is a way by which the child is led to God, who is ready to meet him. It is not a matter of " seeking " God or of " finding " him. Only if he were hidden could he be sought, and unless he were lost there would be no need to find him. The word in Isaiah is a reminder: " I was ready to be sought by those who did not ask for me; I was ready to be found by those who did not seek me " (Isa. 65:1). When worship is seen as encounter, rather than as a simple emotional awareness of wonder through love or beauty, there is a different reason to be concerned with the time and form of worship. Prayers and worship are a meeting between God and man. They are the recognition of encounter on the part of persons, and in that recognition lies the beginning of response.

RECOGNITION AS APPROPRIATION

Response is the recognition through which the person appropriates faith and makes it his own. This is the decision by which the individual accepts responsibility before God. A parallel may be seen in cultural education where it is recognized that learning does not take place until the pupil accepts the activity or experience undertaken. Being aware of the task is not enough; there must also be a willingness to direct one's energies toward its completion.

Response, like encounter, is an individual action in which the Christian community gives encouragement, but in which the individual must make the decision. The response in recognition is seen as faith, hope, and love. Faith is the response to God's love in Jesus Christ and the form in which reconciliation takes place. It is trust in God, through which he is able to indwell a person by the Holy Spirit. The child is able to turn toward adolescence; he is able to accept brothers and sisters at home; he is able to overcome disappointments in school relationships. These are concomitants of his response in faith.

Faith brings hope. Participating in what God has been doing for his people through the generations, the child has assurance of what can be done for him. He is enabled to overcome worry (and little children do worry). He is helped in his insecurities. He can know that God is with him in every moment of his life.

Recognition brings love. The child, knowing God as personal, responds in love. Through participation with the children who saw Jesus, the people who listened to him, and those who watched him at his work of healing, children today know how God loves the world. They cannot love an idea of God, but they can love the God who acts and who is known through his redemptive activity. Children know failure — sometimes by their own standards and sometimes because of the standards imposed upon them by the adult world. Through the gospel message the child learns, even as do adults, that nothing can separate us from the love of God — not "badness" or disobedience, or failure, or unpopularity, or anything else. Repentance brings forgiveness and a new spirit for living.

When encounter has been followed by response, the child willingly becomes a part of the Christian community. This is his outward commitment.[2] This time of decision can occur at any point in a person's life; indeed, it can occur at more than one point.

Until it occurs, a life is not fully integrated, for there is no center to existence and no norm from which to see life whole.

When the child enters into the community, he takes upon himself the promises made in his behalf by his parents at his baptism.[3] He is alone before God, and yet he is in the presence of others who have earlier been called into this same fellowship.[4] He receives the realization of oneness within the community in the action that customarily follows soon upon this new membership, namely, participation in the Holy Communion.

Communication as the Formulation and Expression of Ideas

Communication is the attempt of people to form meaningful relationships with one another. Participation leads to recognition. Recognition seeks a way of expression. The expression is communication.

Response, seen as reverent participation, expresses itself in certain ideas and concepts. This indicates the relationship between *kērygma* and apologetic: the church explains its message to itself and to others. Faith precedes theologizing, as action precedes the description of action. Thus meanings are formulated. The simplest formulation of Christian meanings is to be found in the creeds. Those who repeat the Creed do so, not so much as the avowal of an intellectual formula, but rather as the witness of their faith. Theologizing, seen as communication, has a dynamic quality. The Creed must be appropriated anew by each generation of Christians. Since it has survived nearly fifteen centuries (and its slow formulation grew from the Biblical record), it is hardly likely to be displaced at an early date. Its present omission from the teaching of some churches may be due in part to the fact that it had earlier been presented to children for rote learning—a practice from which this generation rightly has turned away. Creeds and catechisms are ways of explaining faith, and they in turn need to be explained. Parents and teachers explain as they share a mature faith in witness to the children. Pupils explain to one another while they are seeking ever deeper understanding.

The creeds represent philosophical reflection upon the gracious acts of God as these are made known in the Bible. Many children have questions that are answerable in this form. Some people grasp meanings even through abstractions. From Origen to Paul Tillich, the Christian church has always had thinkers who were able to interpret the *kērygma* in philosophical terms.

When this theologizing is seen in the context of the worshiping community, and when it grows out of the *kērygma* in order to explain it, there is little danger of making an idol out of ideas. The abstract conception of God is not a legitimate substitute for what is knowable by the personal self-disclosure of the living, acting God through the Bible, and pre-eminently through Christ. Ideas about Jesus cannot take the place of a commitment to him as the head of the church. Ideals for living and for society will not replace the daily dying and rising by which the presence of Christ is made real in the immediate situation of existence.

Not all communication, however, comes through the sharing of ideas; indeed, there are many people for whom ideas are never important. Salvation is by faith, not intellect. Although Christianity can challenge the most highly gifted intellect, it can be lived with equal devotion by one of small intellectual powers. Symbols are a medium for communicating concepts for some people. They have been used in the church from the beginning. The sign of the fish is theological, in fact, kerygmatic. A symbol is a picturization through which doctrine is explained without being closely defined. A triangle gives an understanding of the Trinity to those who could never read a treatise on the subject. The cross is the center for Christian devotion while theories of the atonement are being discussed by theologians. The use of symbols in Christian education has been recognized in recent years, but the age at which symbols should first be used is still under discussion.

Pupils in Communication

Pupils communicate with one another. They do this in several ways. They encourage one another in the formation of ideas based on reverential participation. Here is the place of conversation and discussion in teaching. Conversation is a sharing of ideas, feelings, and attitudes. It is a way of formulating questions and clarifying insights. " Reverential participation " is important. This is not a way of imposing ideas or of shutting out other ideas. Communication implies sharing. This is the place at which the new emphases in group dynamics become helpful to the teacher and to pupils in an awareness of their own interactions. Group-centered leadership makes it possible for the teacher to share more easily and for the children to question more openly. Small groups and "buzz sessions" give opportunities for even shy children to make attempts at verbalization of their understandings.

Discussion is a way of formulating ideas on a foundation of sources other than the self. Discussion is a disciplining of ideas under the correction of facts. It is one thing to converse about religion, quite another to discuss the Biblical understanding of God. Discussion causes the person to see himself in the context of others who have struggled with the same problems and found some working affirmations. Books enter into discussion, and the Bible in particular; for it makes discussion another way of bringing the remembered past into the contemporary situation. The discussants realize that they are not alone but are surrounded by a great cloud of witnesses.

Witness is a part of the explaining to one another by which pupils teach one another in conversation and discussion. They engage in a sharing of experiences of what God has done. It must be a freely willed response of the child to tell what is meaningful to him. People are not convinced by argument so often as they are by the recital of experience. When the Biblical writers wanted to turn their people back to God, they used this method. They did not warn the people that God was omnipotent, omniscient, and omnipresent. They reminded them that God had made a covenant with them; that he was the God of Abraham, Isaac, and Jacob; and that he had delivered them from Egypt.

Questions are an aid in the formation of ideas, provided they avoid dogmatism, on one side, and prying, on the other. A well-phrased question will help a child to think and to express himself. The church school teacher could learn from the psychological counselor how to ask questions. This is done skillfully by Helen Parkhurst in her radio conversations with children. Miss Parkhurst engages in twenty-minute unrehearsed broadcasts with five or six children who usually are between the ages of nine and twelve. Occasionally younger children participate for the interaction of their point of view with that of the older children. The subjects are matters such as worry, death, God, and prayer — all of them profound. The children's responses are startling in their frankness. The questions are simple, asked in a quiet, unemotional voice.[5] It is a rare church school teacher who even begins to explore the meaning that conversation, discussion, or question and answer can have in helping children to communicate their faith — and their reaching toward faith — with the teacher and with one another.

Pupils further communicate with one another through composition. Such composition could be in the form of music, pictures, drama, or writing in any form. One of the important contributions of progressive education has been the encouragement of such free activities on the part of children. They have been enabled thereby to develop imagination and originality, and have been introduced to ways of expressing their thoughts, feelings, and experiences in tangible form. Psychoanalysis has made a further contribution by the suggestion that such composition need not necessarily express the concrete, but might be an attempt at setting forth the otherwise inexpressible. Teachers could well try to develop some understanding of contemporary art, symbolic poetry, and modern music. "Creative" activities in the church school have not always been as "free" as they might be. More freedom would be given if children were not restricted to the media of paint and crayon. Some might work better in clay, others in music or informal drama, others in the dance, while still others might find an outlet in writing.

"Creative" writing itself takes diversified forms; story, essay, article, poem, meditation, prayer, letter, biographical or autobiographical sketch are but a few of many avenues of expression. Because prayer is a way of communication with God within the fellowship, the preparation of prayers becomes a special concern in teaching. Children can be encouraged to write prayers for their own use, and for use in the group, and be helped to see the difference. The psalms are suggested forms of prayer. The litany is a form sometimes used in church schools, but rarely with the depth the form permits. The collect is almost totally neglected, although it is simple in form while being capable of great diversity of expression. A child who grows up knowing and using the collect form might find it easier to pray in a group. Prayer is the deepest way through which Christians minister to one another. There is no fully existential participation without it.

The encouragement of various forms of communication growing out of reverent recognition and participation in the historic life of the fellowship may have especial importance for the church in this day. There has begun a resurgence of Christian art in contemporary life: in painting, sculpture, music, poetry, drama, novel, and architecture. There is a revival of the religious dance. Such forms can best express the Christian community if they arise from within the community. Christian teachers today have the privilege of encouraging those who will express the *kērygma* in art forms tomorrow. The church cannot merely use the expressions of contemporary life, adapting them to its needs. That has been attempted through all the centuries and found wanting. The dance and the drama both had to leave the church, and the oratorio has always been too operatic for satisfactory use in the church. The dynamic understanding of theology, arising from a renewed awareness of the word of God in the Bible, and especially from a new commitment to the incarnate Word, will make possible new forms of witness. Foundations for these are laid through the present nurture of children in the faith.

PUPILS' SELF-KNOWLEDGE AND SELF-TRANSCENDENCE

The ways of communication among pupils are enhanced as they become old enough to know the self and to transcend the self. This is the time at which the child can begin to feel inde-

pendent because he begins to be aware of himself as an independent entity. The concept of the self has been engaging the
researches of psychologists. It has become apparent that the development of a realistic self-image is one of the tasks of growth.
Self-acceptance is a characteristic that colors a person's reactions
to his situation. As the child grows in the ability to see himself,
he grows also in the ability to transcend the present moment of
time in which he lives. History takes on meaning for him. Space
and time have perspective. He begins to be able to ask what are
called " thought " questions. He sees himself apart from the environing world. The schools explain the meaning of the world to
him in terms of science, and the meaning of himself in terms of
" health."

Self-understanding makes possible self-transcendence. The
child needs to know that he is separate, self-sufficient, and independent. When he is assured of these facts to any degree, he can
take a further step, that of deliberately relating himself to others.
It may be that the truest self-knowledge comes through such relationships. Independence is not true freedom; it is merely aloneness. In voluntarily putting oneself in relationship to other persons,
one finds freedom and adjustment. The child must come to a
time of accepting not only himself but his parents, and even his
brothers and sisters. There are teachers to be accepted, and people who are different from himself. This does not refer to a passive acceptance or toleration, but to a dynamic acceptance, a participation with others.

For the Christian, the only true self-understanding and the
only full adjustment come through relationship to God. This is
expressed in Augustine's often-repeated sentence, " Thou madest
us for thyself, and our heart is restless, until it repose in thee." [6]
In this perspective, the knowledge of God provides ever deeper
knowledge of the self, for the self now has a point of reference.
With the assurance that God accepts one, there can be more security in seeking acceptance by other persons.

Self-transcendence brings also a realization of aloneness that
independence does not bring. The independent person is wrapped

up in himself; the self-transcendent person can know what it is to be separated from other persons and from God. Thus he is enabled to know what "dependence" is in the Christian sense. This is not the helpless dependence to which people sometimes feel themselves reduced by circumstances (which is the child's situation in a world of adults). This is the voluntary dependence of one who accepts a relationship in love, and begins to be aware of the fact that love is a paradoxical situation: it is a joyful bondage which gives the kind of freedom that can come only from that kind of security.

Participation can be understood now, for it is entered into voluntarily. Recognition is made complete, for it is done in full knowledge of the self. Communication can be clear, for the person knows himself in relation to time and space, to the world and other persons, and to God who is the source of his life and his Redeemer.

Personality is thus seen as a dimension of relationship to God, who created it and who continually recreates it by his Holy Spirit as the person responds in faith. In the Bible, young people were often most aware of God's claims on their life. Reference has been made to Samuel. The Gospel writers felt that the child Jesus had an early awareness of his vocation.

If the child has this ability to respond to God, there is a need that faith, rather than moralisms, hold a central place in curriculum. Horace Bushnell made a plea for this over a century ago. He wrote that it is a mistake of teaching when

> "the child is put to the doing of good works, and the making up of a character in the self-regulating way. . . . Nothing will draw the child onward in ways of piety, but the sense of forgivenesses, helps, felt sympathies of grace and love. Salvation by faith is the only kind of religion that a child can support. If there is no ladder to heaven but a ladder of will-works and observances, he will not be climbing it long. Where Luther fell off and lay groaning, infant steps will not persist." [7]

The historical takes on new significance by the understanding of the activity of God in events, and the child has a broader scope for appreciation. He will see this both in the Old Testament records and in the life of Jesus. He will have still further areas of communication with others.

Deeds in Communication

Christian communication also takes place through deeds of loving service. Seemingly there has been a great deal of stress on this point in recent curriculum writing; actually, however, the type of stress requires examination. "Deeds of loving-kindness" do not mean that the child is told he must be helpful because God loves him and expects him to return love in that way. Love is not shown because it is expected, but because the one who loves and feels loved cannot do otherwise. A moralistic stress on "doing to others" may remove the dynamic quality of a freely willed response to God. This danger is always inherent in the attempt to reduce the intangible to a set of suggestions in a lesson book. Christian action is a response in love for God's continuous saving action, and not a requirement to be fulfilled in order to receive that action. Such acts of devoted service are found everywhere in the New Testament — Peter and John healing the man at the Beautiful Gate, Lydia making garments for the poor, small churches gathering a collection for their brethren in Jerusalem. Seemingly these were not world-shaking events, nor were they highly organized efforts. Yet they were a form of witness that made Christ real to the Christians' contemporaries in the Roman Empire, so that many turned to him.

Action happens because, after participation and the recognition of God in faith, there is the attempt to communicate this new life in word and deed. There is an awareness of God's love that one must show toward others. There is a realization that the love of God is not a possession, but a gift; that it cannot be kept, but must be shared; that it is not a static "thing," but a motivating power. Only when a person is in this situation is he capable of truly Christian deeds springing from love. This is never a sentimental, but always an ethical, love.

It can be seen that this *is* the basis for the child's motivation in Christian social action and the world-wide outreach of the church. These will be an integral, inescapable element in all Christian witness, and for that reason will become an essential part of the curriculum. The use of interesting publicity devices, even "experience-centered" ones, to encourage children to give money to a project, is not analagous. Indeed, these may avoid the necessary, and far more difficult, responsibility the church has for its children before God. Acts of devoted service are a way that God gives his people by which to express their love for him and to show forth his love to others.

One gives himself with such a gift. That is the reason it cannot be done as a response to a rule. It is not a requirement, or a way of "learning by doing," but is consequent to the response of the whole self to the redemptive activity of God. Only as the self is a part of the gift can the gift be a way of communication. Existential communication does not involve simple information, but total awareness. This happens when the giver has transcended himself sufficiently to see himself in relation to God and to other persons. In such participation the deeds and the doers in the early Christian community are made contemporary, and the church becomes truly an extension of the incarnation.

Loving action does not involve only the things given, although the feeding of the hungry, the visiting of the sick, and similar charitable actions must never be omitted. The witness that Christians make by teaching is itself an act of devoted service. Persons are the media through whom God chooses to make himself known; thus this mutuality of teaching is a form of love in action through which God encounters persons. When Peter healed the lame man, he said, "I have no silver and gold, but I give you what I have; in the name of Jesus Christ of Nazareth, walk" (Acts 3:6). The gift of Peter took the form of words, but these words were filled with power. Teachers help their pupils to stand up and walk. Christians witnessing to their faith do that for one another and for those who are seeking the way.

Methods for Christian nurture, then, should be life-centered, in the fullest understanding of that term. They will include ways for participation in those historic events in the Bible and the church through which God's saving activity is known. They will include ways by which the child, through such participation, comes into a recognition that God speaks to him here and now and seeks to give him integration of the self through the Holy Spirit in the life of the church. They will include ways by which the child may learn to communicate this fullness of life to others by word and deed.

Focus for the Future

MAKING TEACHING RELEVANT

Teaching arises from the *kērygma* to nurture those who are young in the faith. Where children have grown for years without hearing the story at all, they need to hear the proclamation. In so far as children have their cultural education within a secular framework, they need to be helped to understand the Christian faith through the thought forms with which they are familiar. Recently this has meant giving theistic foundations to a naturalistic view of the world. A deeper appreciation of the meaning of the primary gospel will give the occasion for new thought as to how to make this pertinent within the verbal understandings of the American child.

The nurturing of the young also includes setting forth the moral implications of the gospel, a primary interest in recent curriculum writing, reflected in the type of stories used and in the selection of passages from the Bible for emphasis. Another factor in the Christian education of children has been the interpretation of the proclamation itself in terms of the catechism and the Creed. Groups that traditionally have used these forms are rethinking methods for making them vivid and dynamic by relating their meanings to the life of the child before he comes to an age for memorizing the words.

Contemporary understandings in theology and recent insights in education suggest areas in which the curriculum of the church school may be strengthened as learning is made relevant to the needs of the child within the fellowship of the church.

THE CHURCH IN CURRICULUM

Christian education needs to view the church as the environing center for Christian nurture. This involves a view of the church as the worshiping community. Current curriculum materials have caught the feeling-tone of the church as a fellowship of people rather than as a building or an institution. This is made vivid in reading books for children which help them to feel the warmth and friendliness that are in a church. However, such books do not often make it clear why the people of a church should have this friendliness. One feels that they depict kind and courteous people who know that those who are in a church should show kindness to strangers because Jesus would have done so. Junior courses are usually in the field of church history or are concerned with worship. There is little indication in them that the members of the church are those who have responded to God's work and that their friendliness is a testimony to what he has done and is doing in them and through the church. Although juniors are interested in belonging to small groups (complete with initiations and secret codes), there is no attempt to show them that the church is a group of those who are "called out." The place of Christ in his church and the work of the Holy Spirit are seemingly left for consideration among older boys and girls.

When the church is viewed as the environing center for Christian nurture, there becomes apparent a responsibility for providing the child with a basic security by making him a part of an understanding fellowship. This is accomplished from the child's angle by helping him to feel that the people at church are his friends. One thinks of the tensions that arise between adults and children over noise in the building, damage to the lawn, or disorderliness in rooms, for instance. Children need to be helped to feel that they are a part of the whole church, surrounded by the loving care of the members. Something of this is accomplished in smaller churches when the children are welcomed at parish meals; nor does it seem to be an impossibility even in larger parishes, if the will thereto is vital.

In many churches there is a tendency to exclude children from the church at principal services of worship on the ground of the children's inability to comprehend the service. These have become generally accepted dicta: "The Bible was written for adults," and "Sermons are prepared for adults"; in short, that the service of morning worship is for adult members of the church. The intellectual quality of many Protestant services is a factor here. The sermon is constructed in the form of rational propositions; the pastoral prayer tends to be lengthy and involved; the anthems are complicated. This is no criticism of dignity and order, but is mentioned only to point out the lack of drama and congregational participation, which can tend to make the congregation become an "audience." Children do not always make good audiences. Nevertheless, the basic reality of the church can never be experienced apart from the church at worship. It may be that curriculum materials could prepare children for attendance at part of the morning service, that classes could be encouraged to attend together occasionally, and that families could be encouraged to attend together on at least the great festival days of the church year. This is still an open question meriting and receiving serious consideration, especially with the current emphasis on family participation in the life of the church. It is significant that preparation for attending the church service sometimes appears in a summer curriculum unit, at a time when families have more time together.

Enabling the child to feel that the fellowship of the church is a basic source of security leads to an understanding of the dynamic quality of the church as the body of Christ. There is a living continuity with the first Christians. They are not simply historical figures on whom the church was "built," but participants in "the communion of saints," the invisible church. They are people whom children can love because they too knew Jesus the Lord, people to whom the church today is grateful because they kept the faith in their time. The worshiping community is aware of them at the service of Holy Communion, on All Saints' Day, and on the festival of Pentecost. They can be made real to children by the manner in which a story is written. They are still a living element of the church quite as much as are the children who hear about them.

The testimony of the church to the world today is another factor to be understood for curriculum. There seems in most published curriculum to be little acknowledgment of a difference or contrast between the church's witness and the judgments of the surrounding society. The prevailing emphasis of the church in the United States seems to be that of an accommodation to culture in general, and this is reflected in curriculum material.[1] " Right " and " wrong " are clear in these books. A child may do wrong and regret it. There is no indication that he would win anything but approval by doing right. This seems to show a rather superficial optimism. A child, even of primary age, has had the experience of being criticized by his group for some action that seemed acceptable to him, even of being attacked for some unknown reason or no reason at all — such being the occasional cruelty of children. He is sometimes misunderstood even by those who love him most. He knows the possibility of being hurt for no good reason. The sharpness of the Christian witness is not beyond the appreciation of children. They already have learned that suffering is a part of love. They need the opportunity to sense that there are times in this generation when suffering gives a depth of dimension to faith.

These are elements in an understanding of the church as the environing center for Christian nurture.

THE BIBLE IN CURRICULUM

Christian nurture should take more seriously the insights arising from contemporary Biblical studies. Curriculum materials indicate that the findings of nineteenth-century scholarship regarding textual and source criticism have been integrated into the material. There is a strong concern evidenced that children shall know how the Bible developed, how shepherd life was carried on in ancient Palestine, and how the boy Jesus might have lived. All of these, however, are simply surrounding data for the essential message of the Bible, which scholars today are interpreting as the record of the redeeming activity of the living God through persons in their historical situations.

The teaching of the New Testament could be enriched in several areas through the contributions that form-criticism has made to an understanding about Jesus and the life of the primitive Christian church. There is a recognizable unity in the New Testament as the witness to Jesus as the Lord. This will require some rethinking of the past attempts to separate in children's minds the Jesus of history and the Christ of experience, as well as the concern lest children confuse Jesus and God. It suggests that a place be made in the curriculum where children can be helped to understand the work of the Holy Spirit through the life of the church.[2] There are educational problems in deciding what children understand at different ages, but there are also problems involved in making Jesus an ordinary person in the teaching of primary and even junior age children and then trying later to introduce him as the Lord of life. It may be said that the regnant viewpoint concerning Jesus as the great prophet and example has been as much responsible for the dichotomy in teaching as has been the children's ability at comprehension. The final result tends to be a unitarian-Jewish understanding of God, rather than the fullness of the trinitarian apprehension which has been the distinguishing mark of the classical Christian faith.

Form-criticism provides some new understandings with regard to both the words and work of Jesus. The writers of the Gospels knew him as the One who had been sent by God to show the likeness of God, to save people from sin and to give them new life. His words and his example — the life and teachings — were for those who had responded in repentance. The Kingdom had come in his person for those who were willing to receive it. Rationalizing is an inadequate method for interpreting the Gospels. Certain incidents may be factual or legendary, but as they stand they constitute the only extant records of the early church. While some reading books for children are trying to incorporate these newer insights, there is in others a considerable emphasis on moralizing about Jesus, on presenting him only as a kind and helpful person who told people about God's love and taught them how to live in love toward one another. There is little indication that Jesus, in his person, showed what God is like, or that Jesus had any awareness that his call by God and the power of the Holy Spirit within him had any uniqueness, although the Gospels seem to portray this as the case.

Such stories lack an indication of what it was in persons that made it possible for Jesus to help them. The narratives are written in such a way that the reader tends to identify with Jesus and to be brought to the understanding that he must be kind and helpful as Jesus was. But if the primary witness of the Gospels is to how Jesus enables persons to follow him, then it might be better if stories were so slanted that the reader identified with the persons whom Jesus helped. Something of this is found in the illustrations used in some storybooks. If Jesus is shown in the background, or the reader is presented with a side view of him, or if he is shown as looking at the people, the reader sees in terms of those who are confronted by Jesus.[8]

Contemporary Biblical studies have a further insight for Christian education in the understanding of the *kērygma* and the *didachē*. To use their insights would require some refocusing of the emphases in teaching. The *kērygma,* as the central proclamation, should be primary. Current teaching materials, however, have avoided the word " gospel " and tended to give inadequate explanations of what the " good news " really is. This is particularly noticeable when it is presented as a way of life or as new rules for living, for this completely misses the point of the gracious activity of God toward men. Materials that attempt to deal with the meaning of the gospel sometimes show a confusion between the meaning of the *kērygma* and that of the moral teaching derived from it.

The recognition of the place of the *kērygma* puts a new emphasis on the activity by which Jesus changed lives. His healings were more than helpfulness. They were made possible by a person's faith in him and they resulted in a new direction to life. Jesus is not portrayed in the New Testament as having come to teach ideas or to proclaim convictions; rather, he manifested the loving power of God; and what happened to him demonstrated man's rejection of God. Two approaches are contrasted, however, in full awareness that each generation makes its interpretation of Jesus with a concern that he shall be meaningful to people, and there is an inevitable modernization which the next generation tries to correct in its own way. The contribution of nineteenth-century scholarship to curriculum has already been made; the insights of twentieth-century scholarship are just entering curriculum. It is not yet apparent what further changes will be forthcoming during the years ahead.

The emphasis on the *kērygma* is not intended to be made at the expense of an interpretation of the *didachē*. Christian faith is made known in a way of life, and Christians are those who follow Jesus. At the same time, it is important that " living the law of love " shall not be written to mean a self-help discipline by which character is developed. *Didachē* includes broader implications than the rules for the Christian life, important as these are. It includes an understanding of the beliefs of the church, the teaching that arises from the *kērygma* itself. Here are included the historic confessions of faith, the catechisms, and the articles of religion. Any formal creedal teaching, even of the Apostles' Creed, is considered to be beyond the understanding of young children, but stories, conversations, and discussions should be concerned with an understanding of God, who Jesus is, the work of God's Holy Spirit, the forgiveness of sins, the church, and the life everlasting. These come within the experience of children and will require thoughtful attention. A broader understanding of the teaching will be reflected in the passages chosen from the Bible, in the prayers used for worship, and in the hymns that are learned.

Some curriculum units that present the work of the church have this wider emphasis. The World Council of Churches is seen through the eyes of children. World friendship units are beginning to be slanted in the direction of seeing missionary activity in terms of lives changed through the power of God rather than simply as works of good will by which a better social and economic life is achieved. Excellent use is made of fine hymns of praise, but there seems to be considerable hesitancy in introducing children to the church's hymns in praise of Jesus as the Lord. While the rich resources of liturgical prayers are for the most part closed to the children of the nonliturgical churches, there are units of study on the Lord's Prayer. Such examples point to a direction, even though they may not yet hold the proportionate place they might within the writings for children.

Relationship Between God and Man in Curriculum

Christian education needs to reconsider its view of the relationship between God and man. Contemporary psychology, philosophy, and literature point to the situation of modern man. Education has been concerned with the child's anxieties, his need for love, security, and approval. This has not yet been reflected to any extent in the curriculum materials of the church school.[4] The kindergarten child depicted in the usual story seldom gives any indication of anxiety, hostility, or insecurity. The emphasis is not on how he feels but on what he does, and there is no implication as to the motivation for what he does. Normally the conflict arises because he refuses to share a toy or forgets to be helpful, but a positive suggestion helps him to remedy this momentary lapse and a Bible verse or a "thank-you" prayer brings the story to an inspirational close.

When the present curriculum for the Presbyterian Church U.S.A. first appeared, it included a book called *Davie Decides*.[5] The story followed a five-year-old boy through a whole week. On each day his own deliberate action was followed by some misfortune which resulted in his individual methods of expressing hostilities. Children did not seem to object to the book, nor did their mothers, but some professional religious educators considered the book too negative. Now every mother knows, and so does every child, that such situations arise at least once in every day. The story was true to life. At the same time, from the standpoint of story construction, it probably reiterated the conflict too consistently, especially in view of the fact that this was a reading book to be used chapter by chapter, week by week. Nevertheless it was an attempt to view daily living through the eyes of a child and to find the solution to his problems in religious terms. The book has been withdrawn and replaced with *Time for Tommy*.[6] Tommy has just one deliberate act of wrongdoing: he stops the clock in order to have more time for play. As a result he is late for kindergarten, he misses important events, he gets angry, his mother is late preparing lunch, and his father is late for work. Tommy learns that time is a part of God's purpose for human existence and that any attempt to set oneself against the purpose of God leads only to frustration and unhappiness. In the words of Ecclesiastes, or The Preacher, "For everything there is a season, and a time for every matter under heaven" (Eccl. 3:1). Tommy's motives and reactions, however, are simpler than Davie's and do not suggest the deeper range of the latter's emotions.

In most curriculum materials attempts at probing the existential depths of a child's experience fade from sight in the primary materials, and junior characters are scarcely more than types. Story-writing becomes entirely expository. Without being so obviously didactic as were nineteenth-century stories, they are nonetheless moralistic.

The Bible has a realistic view of man. Man is made in the image of God and meant to be a child of God, but he has deliberately sinned, turning from God to live for and by himself like a willful child, sure of his own strength. The gospel is God's answer to man's need. Here is another basic experience, understandable on a completely human plane. Children turn aside to their own ways; love alone can give them the security through which they are enabled to grow into loving and kindly persons. When they do not live in a family where they receive love, they may sense the need for it and respond to the love of God as it is made known to them. Even children in loving homes know what it means to feel estranged, and these have experienced the relief of reunion in a forgiving love which helps and heals.

" The grace of God " is a phrase that has been given no place in the writing for children, yet it is the only term in the English language that makes possible an understanding of the differentiation between the love of God and human love. The avoidance of the distinctive words expressive of the Christian faith and experience makes it difficult to convey the fullness of their meaning to children. Children hear abstract words, even in kindergarten — words such as love, kindness, helpfulness, all of which are interpreted in terms of their activity. The great words that express the good news — grace, faith, trust, repentance — are seldom interpreted in any way, even to children of junior age. This is not a suggestion that abstract theological terms be fed to children, but that the makers of curriculum ask how these essential words of the Christian vocabulary can be put into action so that a whole dimension of Christian living shall not be hidden from growing children at an age when everyday life is broadening their experience in many directions.

The Biblical view of man makes it plain that the encounter between God and man is a decisive event, although it need not necessarily be remembered as a moment of crisis. This is understandable through the relationship of human beings with one another. Two people work side by side, yet at some moment discover that they love each other. Neighbors who live near one another or children who are in the same classroom differentiate particular persons who become close friends. This is not chance; it involves an element of choice. Because the Bible understands God as a personality and not as an abstract power of love and goodness, his relationships with men necessitate a deliberate turning of the person to God in love and trust. Such an understanding requires a rethinking of the evolutionary theory of Christian discipleship. Horace Bushnell's opening sentence to the effect that a child should grow up a Christian and never know himself to have been otherwise was not meant to preclude a personal decision, as the rest of *Christian Nurture* indicates. He was simply objecting to the assertion that a child had to grow up sinful in order to become a converted Christian, as some evangelists of his day were insisting. The first disciples were called and they responded. Christian nurture, if it is to carry out this Biblical understanding, would be seen as helping the child so to grow that he can hear the call and answer it affirmatively, neither ignoring the voice of God nor turning from him in unwillingness to accept the responsibility he offers.

Doubtless the hesitancy that is felt in facing the possibility of individual confrontation with its necessity for decision lies partly in the background of persons who have been trained in religious education during the past thirty years. Some came from a religiously conservative background, and breathed free air in the possibility that religious growth could be a gradual development. They remembered guilt, fear, and turmoil, and they turned from these with relief. But the new answer was too easy a solution. There is a depth of reality involved in the making of a decision. The decision to be led by God and to confess Christ as Lord affects all the other decisions of life. The cost is hardly paid at all in the beginning, but the assurance of the immanent Holy Spirit is already granted in the decision itself.

There comes a moment in a life when God is no longer simply a word or an idea but a living reality whom the person recognizes. This may happen to a child at any age; it is the beginning of his relationship personally with God. It is also the beginning of the child's understanding of the love of God and of what it means to trust God. This is the time at which prayer becomes real. The decision that leads the child into the adult membership of the church comes later. This relationship makes the difference between " joining " the church, as though it were an institution, and uniting with the living body of Christ, the worshiping community.

Current materials for children give little hint of such understanding of the relationship between God and the child, although junior reading books contain material pointing toward church membership. These are usually aimed in the direction of giving rational explanations to various facets of church life, or they are designed to help the child in understanding the elements in a service of worship, or they try to explore what it means to be a Christian. The apprehension that God meets persons in particular situations may be difficult to convey, but the possibilities have hardly even been explored. Few would wish to return to the obvious evangelistic methods from which parts of the church revolted, nor can a relationship be established by promotional means. The Holy Spirit works as he wills, and human beings can only be channels through whom God may make himself known. The teacher's own relationship to God shows through his use of every page of written curriculum. Biblical characters often may speak to this need better than do stories from child experience. A child might avoid identifying with an obvious reference, but find meaning through the story of Abraham, Samuel, Isaiah, or Paul. It is not enough to assume that because kindergarten children have been taught to say "thank-you" prayers, or because teachers have been alerted to be aware of moments of spontaneous worship within the group, that any particular child has known life's most important experience: that of recognizing God, who has sought him in love and mercy.

This leads into an element that has been characteristic of recent curriculum materials: the emphasis on finding God in nature. There is a distinction to be noted between seeing God in his world and knowing God revealed through his world. There were nature religions in the ancient world, but people turned to Christianity because it was different. When children are told that the beauties of the springtime world reveal God's love, the embarrassing problem of evil in the world immediately presents itself. Here is where the gospel answers that God's love and care are first and most surely known in the Person of Jesus Christ. The world of "nature" can be viewed meaningfully in Christian terms only from this context. Christ has overcome evil, sin, and death. God works his purposes toward those who love him through storms, famines, and illness. God does not accommodate himself to "nature"; he is the Lord and the Creator of the whole world.

Much curriculum material gives an erroneous interpretation of the life of Jesus in this connection. In the first place, he is presented as a lover of nature. The story of the soils is used as a picture of a farmer's life with no hint of the interpretation of the parable. This is done on the thesis that the child is too young to understand the interpretation. To tear the story from its context is an uncritical use of the Bible. The story of the mustard seed is similarly distorted. The teaching about God's care, from the Sermon on the Mount, is presented fairly, but Jesus' ending, "Seek first his kingdom and his righteousness" (Matt. 6:33), is usually omitted.

The second place in which curriculum material tends to distort the New Testament understanding is in the teaching for Easter. This festival is linked with the awakening of plant life in the spring. The omission of the story of the resurrection usually grows out of the question as to the age at which a child can comprehend it. (There is also the question as to the age at which anyone comprehends it. Mystery is an element that keeps the Christian faith from being a set of propositions.) Sometimes there are attempts at rationalizing the experience of the disciples with the thought that the spirit of Jesus is alive and triumphant in the world.

The objection, however, is not to the age at which children are introduced to the resurrection story so much as to the use of nature material at Easter time. This is confusing, and connects with the festival a non-Biblical element which is closer to paganism than to Christianity. If the *kērygma* were central in a curriculum, stories of Jesus would be used at Easter time and units about God's world would be taught elsewhere. There is no parallel between the resurrection of Jesus and the growth of tulips in the spring. The connection would have no meaning to children living in the Southern hemisphere. Nor is the Easter event equivalent to any Greek conception of immortality. This is a caution about using ideas with very young children that will make it difficult for them, later on, to appreciate the event that is basically meaningful for Christian faith. The resurrection, as the culmination of the crucifixion, is a part of the *kērygma,* and is vital for the new relationship that Jesus brought between God and man.

Communication involves facts other than methodology and material. There are deep levels to communication. Persons are involved in their interactions with one another. God is involved, and the work of the Holy Spirit is not under the direction of mortal man by any technique. It is not always the perfection of methods but the sincerity of outreach that counts in Christian nurture. Persons play a part in the efficacy of their methods. Persons are channels of communication, through their witness in the life of the church, the family, and the community. Something of this is recognized in curriculum suggestions that visitors come to a class: missionaries, members of the church, or community helpers. They come, however, to explain their work rather than to testify to the motivations for their activity. Sometimes the person himself will break through the barrier. This seems to happen more often when converts are speaking, members of the younger churches who find themselves in the presence of children who have never known anything but Christian homes and the Christian church. Such was a young woman from India who had found release from fear in the knowledge of God's love shown by missionary teachers through the stories of Jesus. Invited to visit a church school class in this country, she tried to convey something of the feelings of her childhood and the joy that had come into her life through Christian faith.

These are factors in communication outside the written curriculum of which those who prepare such courses of study should be aware. A dynamic understanding of the nature of communication will affect methodology, particularly in the direction of showing more awareness of intangible factors. " Experience " is not feeling alone; nor is it only action. That is why the word " existential " is being substituted in an effort to get beyond the inadequacy of the popular understanding of " experience."

THE UNDERSTANDING OF CHRISTIAN CONDUCT

Christian education needs to rethink its understanding concerning the teaching of Christian conduct. Some distortions have grown out of a seemingly overemphasized view of the teachings of Jesus as a " new law." This point of view has made it possible to abstract particular sayings of Jesus from their theocentric context and set them alongside the words of other teachers, thus making him one of the great world reformers. The teachings of Jesus were not unique, as this synthesizing tendency makes apparent. Their uniqueness, in so far as they can be described as being unique, lies in the fact that they were standards of living for those who had been born again. As such they are indeed unique. They were not self-help regulations after the manner of Stoic or Buddhist teachings. One can go through any number of published units of study and find that moralism is the one facet of the *didachē* that finds a place in church school curriculum. It is often a surface moralism in terms of " sharing " and " being helpful." Bible stories are slanted in this direction. Zacchaeus is presented as a man who learned to be friendly; the feeding of the multitude is interpreted in terms of a little boy who shared his lunch. Bible verses are selected to emphasize this point: " Be kind to one another " (Eph. 4:32); " Even a child makes himself known by his acts " (Prov. 20:11); " He went about doing good " (Acts 10:38). The wonder of Jesus' impact on the totality of a human life is blunted by the emphasis on the teaching which was only a part of the encounter. It is even suggested that his works of healing were done in order that people might also hear what he had to say.

The emphasis on the human element in Christian character tends to ignore the divine initiative. Kindergarten children are taught to pray in terms of thanksgiving, yet they are expected to live with an increasing degree of co-operation which only the grace of God could make possible. Sometimes the moral teaching in a curriculum is embodied in stories that show no Christian rootage whatever, and that could be used equally well in a school curriculum stressing moral values. These are stories about well-known or little-known people who have been unselfish, co-operative, and heroic in other ways. It is difficult to teach the moral implications of the Christian faith to children without being too overtly " didactic," and it is seldom even attempted. It may be that fruitful writing in this area will come through stories that use Biblical material in juxtaposition with the child's motivations and actions.

Another element in the stress on moralism is observable in the reflections in curriculum of the middle-class character of our " mainstream " Protestant denominations. Daddy usually wears a business suit in the illustrations employed. Pretty children romp on suburban lawns and quarrel over tricycles. Attractively dressed mothers remove food from well-stocked refrigerators. Here is another factor for the consideration of those who plan and write curriculum for the church school.

A corrective for a one-sided view of the Christian way of life may be derived from an understanding of the relationship between the *kērygma* and the *didachē*. God's redemptive action precedes deeds of Christian love and yields the power to do such deeds. This is the element that has been lacking in church school teaching. The implication has been that all children in the church would know that God loved them because he put them in a beautiful world and gave them loving parents to care for them. As a result, they would want to show their love for him by being kind and helpful. God would help them in their need, but God needs them to help him too. In place of such a misunderstanding there is needed an interpretation with children of God's continually re-creative work by his Holy Spirit, for here is the dynamic for Christian love in action.

Loving service is the glad response in thanksgiving for what God does. In the kerygmatic understanding, this does not refer so much to God's gifts in his world or in human love and care as to his redeeming activity in the lives of persons and in the life of the church. Curriculum stories stress the former but have tended to neglect the latter factor. This is found in some of the

Biblical narratives when they are presented in their own context: Zacchaeus, the woman with her gift of ointment, or the leper who was healed. The teaching materials accompanying these stories do not always appreciate this factor, particularly pertinent on the junior level, when children feel entangled in situations from which they need release in order to do the good that they want to do.

Christian living, the "imitation of Christ," is a form of witness and a way of communicating the Christian faith to others. When Jesus says, "If any one forces you to go one mile, go with him two miles" (Matt. 5:41), the disciples' response in this situation is a glad obedience to the gospel. The life that God has redeemed is given freely to a person to be lived at God's directon and in his full service. Here is an area for experimentation in both story-telling and conversation. It suggests an element of teaching that should have serious attention in the presentation of "giving" projects for children. Love for God has seemed academic as it is met on the pages of teachers' guidebooks. Perhaps words alone cannot carry the meaning of the personal response to the gospel. Curriculum needs construction at this point.

EXISTENTIAL METHODS FOR CURRICULUM

Christian education needs to develop existential methods for teaching. This necessity arises from the newer Biblical studies. The Bible and the theology arising from it are being understood dynamically. Teaching that is simply a recital of facts will not carry the power of the gospel, however vividly the facts are told. A model of a Palestinian village will not awaken faith or sustain it. Plans for a "program" would need for their purpose, not a demonstration of what has been learned, but an expression of that which has been most fully experienced. A worship service would be planned, not to arouse "feelings" of worship, but actually to share in worship together. An examination of the influence of Egyptian ideas on Moses, or an analysis of the primitive quality of the "idea" of God may be valid for scholars but misses that which the writers of the Bible seemingly intended to convey when they told the story in Exodus. It is possible, in the interests of "scientific" teaching, to miss the forest for the trees.

Pragmatic methods are helpful but are not penetrating enough. They have tended to focus largely on rational deductions and the subsequent actions. A kindergarten session might be centered on the experience of "taking turns." This will be emphasized through informal play, a story illustrating the idea, conversation with illustrations from the play period, a worship time that would include a song called "Friends" and the verse "Be kind to one another." Such a session nowhere faces the fact that taking turns may *not* be fun, and the session runs so smoothly in one direction that a child who was not lulled into an acceptance of the proposition would startle a well-prepared teacher by his negativeness.

Pragmatic methods have limitations for appreciating the place of the historical within education, for they view history largely in terms of its present functional value. History cannot be "put in its place." It keeps coming into the present moment as a reminder of what people are and of what they have been. The beginnings of the church are a part of the present church, just as the deliverance of Israel from Egypt is a part of Israel's (and the church's) present existence.

A new methodology is indicated when the Bible is taken seriously as the Word of God to man. While an appreciation of the sociology of Biblical times may increase the child's ability to recreate the situation in imagination, the procedure can be carried so far that historic understanding becomes the main purpose. This is a tendency found less often in the materials of certain "conservative" groups, whose courses of study, on the other hand, sometimes err in the direction of a woodenly propositional treatment of other factors.

"Historical remembrance" refers not so much to putting oneself in the physical situation of Biblical people as to experiencing what they experienced in the pivotal moments of existence; of being one with them in their hopes and fears, in their realization of sin and forgiveness, in their apprehension of the love and mercy of God. It means realizing that the New Testament is grounded in the Old Testament, and that the church is, in a sense, the continuation of the people of Israel, called by God. A child can understand Joseph's boasting without knowing that he lived in a tent or that the long coat was a sign of honor usually accorded the eldest son. In much Biblical teaching, environmental factors are interesting but not necessary.

The selection of Biblical passages is another consideration with regard to curriculum. There is a slight trend toward using longer passages of Scripture with children. They are invited to listen, to enjoy, and to appreciate, with full awareness that they will not completely grasp the meaning. The child can begin to understand that the Bible says many things. It suggests words for praise and prayer, gives guidance for living, and speaks the assurance that God loves and cares. A reading from the Bible might be prefaced with the words, " What does this say to you? " instead of the more customary question, " What do you think this means? " Micah's words may have been spoken in a particular context, but when a group of children have learned all about that, they have merely buried the Biblical record in ancient history. It is at least as important to know what word God can be speaking through Micah to this generation, and to this particular hearer. This is deeper than modernizing, more probing than merely applying the words of the Bible. The full implications of this consideration still await exploration in curriculum writing.

A dynamic approach to the Christian faith requires creative activities as avenues of communication among learners. This has been implicit in curriculum writing for many years, but an examination of the session outlines in almost any course of study raises questions. Many of the so-called " creative " activities are actually constructive activities. Popular handbooks on the subject likewise deal with constructive activities such as building a Palestinian village, making gifts for a friend, or compiling a scrapbook. " Creative " activity results when words, ideas, or experiences have made their impact on a person and he expresses them in some way of which he is capable. This is not so much "illustrative" as "expressive." If a group of children were to talk about the story of Jesus and the children, or to hear verses from Ps. 100, they would need to express the meaning these had for them. Not everyone expresses his thoughts in conversation. Some might wish to write (or dictate to a teacher), others to draw or paint, and still others to work in clay. These activities could be carried out by individuals or in groups. A rereading of the book that has been basic in the education of professional workers in religious education for many years, *Others Call It God,*[1] indicates that present practice has fallen far short of what this teacher did with her group of children in the way of encouraging them to use various media for the concrete expression of thought and feeling. What was "handwork" thirty years ago is still handwork; but it is more elaborate than it used to be.

Free drawing is a customary part of any unit, but it is usually directed toward the depiction of the outward events of a story. Newer understandings about the child, coupled with an awareness of the place of the Bible in human life, could make possible some experiments in freer expression with young children. Symbolism has more of a place in the emotional life of the child than has sometimes been acknowledged, and the meanings of the Christian faith lend themselves to this kind of interpretation.

Creative drama might be used more skillfully, especially with junior children. When children retell a Bible story in their own language, they relive that life. They need to understand the person in a story through empathy in order to re-create him. Thus they can sense the relevance of the Biblical narrative for their own lives.

Children share with one another in writing. The Bible may speak to them in terms of poetry, stories, or prayers. They may find themselves making psalms — not in imitation of the psalms of the Bible, but as an expression of their own praise and prayer.

These creative activities may take final form in a constructed activity: the picture may become a "movie" or fit into a time line; the stories may become a book; the psalms and prayers may be used in the worship of the group. Their prior purpose, however, has not been to fit into a form, but to express to the children themselves what the Bible says to them and what the Christian faith is beginning to mean to them.

The proclamation of the good news that God has come into human life to save his people in a new and wonderful way through Jesus Christ is as living a message today as it was when first spoken. All the teaching that arises from it shares in its vitality. But the teaching must remain rooted in the proclamation. The teaching too is good news. Only dynamic methods can fully carry it so that the work of bringing light and life to men may continue. Periodically those responsible for the teaching work of the church need to check their methods and materials against contemporary ecumenical understanding of the needs of the people for whom it was given and to whom it is addressed. Thus is fulfilled the command of the Lord, "You shall be my witnesses" (Acts 1:8).

Bibliography

NOTE: The reader will have observed that this book takes cognizance of trends in several departments of thought and life, which have been interpreted as having an essential connection with one another as the background for the understanding of the dynamics of Christian education, in both the teaching and learning aspects. Five of these areas stand out as being particularly relevant: the Biblical, educational, literary and philosophical, psychological and sociological, and theological. This is indeed a broad base on which to seek to integrate the viewpoints that concern the Christian educator. Yet it is only by looking at the more significant thinking in all these fields that one can arrive at a viewpoint that can speak relevantly to our modern age. Below are listed some of the works that can be commended to anyone who would like to pursue some of these separate fields more thoroughly. These works are not by any means the only worthy ones available. Yet it is hoped that the list is suggestive of the richness of thought which is the sort of mine from which the Christian pastor, teacher, and leader can dig advantageously.

BIBLICAL

Bowman, John Wick; and Tapp, Roland W., *The Gospel from the Mount.* The Westminster Press, 1957.

Bultmann, Rudolf, *Theology of the New Testament,* tr. by Kendrick Grobel. Charles Scribner's Sons. Vol. 1, 1951; Vol. 2, 1955.

Carrington, Philip, *The Primitive Christian Catechism:* A Study in the Epistles. Cambridge University Press, 1940.

Cullmann, Oscar, *Baptism in the New Testament,* tr. by J. K. S. Reid. Henry Regnery Company, 1950.

———— *Christ and Time:* The Primitive Christian Conception of

Time and History, tr. by Floyd V. Filson. The Westminster Press, 1950.

———— *The Earliest Christian Confessions,* tr. by J. K. S. Reid. Lutterworth Press, London, 1949.

Dibelius, Martin, *Jesus,* tr. by Charles B. Hedrick and Frederick C. Grant. The Westminster Press, 1949.

Dodd, C. H., *The Apostolic Preaching and Its Developments.* Harper & Brothers, 1936.

———— *Gospel and Law:* The Relation of Faith and Ethics in Early Christianity. Columbia University Press, 1951.

———— *History and the Gospel.* Charles Scribner's Sons, 1938.

Farmer, Herbert H., " The Bible, Its Significance and Authority," *The Interpreter's Bible,* ed. by George Arthur Buttrick, Vol. 1. Abingdon Press, 1952.

Filson, Floyd V., *Jesus Christ, the Risen Lord.* Abingdon Press, 1956.

———— *The New Testament Against Its Environment.* Henry Regnery Company, 1950.

Grant, Frederick C., *An Introduction to New Testament Thought.* Abingdon Press, 1952.

Major, H. D. A.; Manson, T. W.; and Wright, C. J., *The Mission and Message of Jesus.* E. P. Dutton & Co., Inc., 1938.

Minear, Paul Sevier, *Eyes of Faith:* A Study in the Biblical Point of View. The Westminster Press, 1946.

———— *The Kingdom and the Power:* An Exposition of the New Testament Gospel. The Westminster Press, 1950.

Mowinckel, Sigmund, *He That Cometh.* Abingdon Press, 1956.

Selwyn, Edward Gordon, *The First Epistle of St. Peter.* The Macmillan Company, London, 1947.

Stauffer, Ethelbert, *New Testament Theology.* The Macmillan Company, 1956.

Taylor, Vincent, *The Atonement in New Testament Teaching.* The Epworth Press, London, 1940.

Wright, G. Ernest, *God Who Acts.* Henry Regnery Company, 1952.

EDUCATIONAL

Benne, Kenneth D.; and Muntyan, Bozidar, *Human Relations in Curriculum Change.* Harper & Brothers, 1950.

Brubacher, John S., ed., *Eclectic Philosophy of Education:* A Book of Readings. Prentice-Hall, Inc., 1951.

_____ *Modern Philosophies of Education*. McGraw-Hill Book Co., Inc., 1950.

_____ *The Public Schools and Spiritual Values* (Seventh Yearbook of the John Dewey Society). Harper & Brothers, 1944.

Bushnell, Horace, *Christian Nurture*. Yale University Press, 1950.

Childs, John L., *Education and Morals:* An Experimentalist Philosophy of Education. Appleton-Century-Crofts, Inc., 1950.

Counts, George S., *Education and American Civilization*. Bureau of Publications, Teachers College, Columbia University, 1952.

Davies, Rupert E., ed., *An Approach to Christian Education*. Philosophical Library, 1956.

Dewey, John, *Democracy and Education:* An Introduction to the Philosophy of Education. The Macmillan Company, 1932.

Division of Christian Education, National Council of the Churches of Christ in the U.S.A., *A Guide for Curriculum in Christian Education*. National Council of the Churches of Christ in the U.S.A., 1955.

Dix, Lester, *A Charter for Progressive Education*. Bureau of Publications, Teachers College, Columbia University, 1939.

Educational Policies Commission, *Moral and Spiritual Values in the Public Schools*. National Education Association of the United States and the American Association of School Administrators, 1951.

_____ *The Purposes of Education in American Democracy*. National Education Association of the United States and the American Association of School Administrators, 1938.

Fahs, Sophia Lyon, *The Old Story of Salvation*. The Beacon Press, Inc., for the Starr King Press, 1955.

Fisk, Margaret Palmer, *The Art of the Rhythmic Choir:* Worship Through Symbolic Movement. Harper & Brothers, 1950.

Forsyth, Nathaniel F., ed., *The Minister and Christian Nurture*. Abingdon Press, 1957.

Fuller, Edmund, ed., *The Christian Idea of Education*. Yale University Press, 1957.

Gutzke, Manford George, *John Dewey's Thought and Its Implications for Christian Education*. King's Crown Press, 1956.

Institute for Religious Education, *Lumen Vitae* (a journal published by a Roman Catholic organization; contains many illuminating articles on the development in that communion of interrelationships between Biblical theology and Christian education). Published in English at Brussels, Belgium.

Jaarsma, Cornelius, ed., *Fundamentals in Christian Education:* Theory and Practice. Wm. B. Eerdmans Publishing Company, 1953.

Jacks, M. L., *The Education of Good Men.* Victor Gollancz, Ltd., London, 1955.

————— *Total Education.* Routledge & Kegan Paul, Ltd., London, 1950.

Jeffreys, M. V. C., *Beyond Neutrality:* Five Essays on the Purpose of Education. Pitman Publishing Corporation, London, 1955.

————— *Education — Christian or Pagan?* University of London Press, London, 1946.

————— *Glaucon:* An Inquiry Into the Aims of Education. Pitman Publishing Corporation, London, 1950.

Kean, Charles Duell, *The Christian Gospel and the Parish Church.* The Seabury Press, Inc., 1953.

Kilpatrick, William Heard, *Philosophy of Education.* The Macmillan Company, 1951.

Lobingier, Elizabeth M., *Activities in Child Education.* The Pilgrim Press, 1950.

Miller, Randolph Crump, *Biblical Theology and Christian Education.* Harper & Brothers, 1956.

————— *The Clue to Christian Education.* Charles Scribner's Sons, 1952.

————— *Education for Christian Living.* Prentice-Hall, Inc., 1956.

Mitchell, Lucy Sprague, *Our Children and Our Schools:* A Picture and Analysis of How Today's Public School Teachers Are Meeting the Challenge of New Knowledge and New Cultural Needs. Simon and Schuster, Inc., 1951.

Munro, Harry C., *Protestant Nurture.* Prentice-Hall, Inc., 1956.

Murray, A. Victor, *Education Into Religion.* Harper & Brothers, 1953.

————— *Teaching the Bible:* Especially in Secondary Schools. Cambridge University Press, 1955.

Peel, E. A., *The Psychological Basis of Education.* Oliver & Boyd, Ltd., Edinburgh, 1956.

Politella, Joseph, *Religion in Education:* An Annotated Bibliography. American Association of Colleges for Teacher Education, 1956.

Prescott, Donald, ed., *Helping Teachers Understand Children.* Commission on Teacher Education, American Council on Education, 1945.

Smart, James D., *The Teaching Ministry of the Church*. The Westminster Press, 1954.

Smith, H. Shelton, *Faith and Nurture*. Charles Scribner's Sons, 1942.

Vieth, Paul H., ed., *The Church and Christian Education*. Published for the Cooperative Publishing Association by The Bethany Press, 1947.

Ward, Winifred, *Playmaking with Children from Kindergarten Through Junior High School* (2d ed.). Appleton-Century-Crofts, Inc., 1957.

Wyckoff, D. Campbell, *The Task of Christian Education*. The Westminster Press, 1955.

LITERARY-PHILOSOPHICAL

Buber, Martin, *I and Thou,* tr. by Ronald Gregor Smith. T. & T. Clark, Edinburgh, 1937.

Butterfield, Herbert, *Christianity and History*. Charles Scribner's Sons, 1950.

Dearmer, Percy; Williams, Vaughan; and Shaw, Martin, eds., *The Oxford Book of Carols*. Oxford University Press, London, 1928.

Geren, Paul, *Burma Diary*. Harper & Brothers, 1943.

Hopper, Stanley Romaine, ed., *Spiritual Problems in Contemporary Literature*. Published for the Institute of Religious and Social Studies, Harper & Brothers, 1952.

Jaspers, Karl, *The Perennial Scope of Philosophy,* tr. by Ralph Manheim. Philosophical Library, Inc., 1949.

Marcel, Gabriel, *Being and Having,* tr. by Katharine Farrar. The Dacre Press, London, 1949.

Martin, P. W., *Experiment in Depth:* A Study of the Work of Jung, Eliot, and Toynbee. Routledge & Kegan Paul, Ltd., London, 1955.

Roberts, David Everett, *Existentialism and Religious Belief*. Oxford University Press, 1957.

Tillich, Paul, *The Courage to Be*. Yale University Press, 1952.

Wedel, Theodore O., *The Christianity of Main Street*. The Macmillan Company, 1950.

Wilder, Amos N., *Modern Poetry and the Christian Tradition:* A Study in the Relation of Christianity to Culture. Charles Scribner's Sons, 1952.

PSYCHOLOGICAL-SOCIOLOGICAL

Baruch, Dorothy Walter, *New Ways in Discipline:* You and Your Child Today. Whittlesley House-McGraw Hill Book Co., Inc., 1949.

———— *One Little Boy.* Julian Press, Inc., 1952.

Bonthius, Robert H., *Christian Paths to Self-acceptance.* King's Crown Press, 1948.

Boyd, Malcolm, *Crisis in Communication:* A Christian Examination of the Mass Media. Doubleday & Co., Inc., 1957.

Breckenridge, Marian Edgar; and Vincent, E. Lee, *Child Development:* Physical and Psychological Growth Through the School Years. W. B. Saunders Company, 1949.

Guntrip, Henry, *Psychotherapy and Religion.* Harper & Brothers, 1957.

Havighurst, Robert J., *Developmental Tasks and Education.* Longmans, Green & Co., Inc., 1950.

Hymes, James, *Understanding Your Child.* Prentice-Hall, Inc., 1952.

Jenkins, Gladys; Shacter, Helen; and Bauer, William, *These Are Your Children.* Scott, Foresman and Company, 1949.

Jersild, Arthur T., *In Search of Self:* An Exploration of the Role of the School in Promoting Self-understanding. Bureau of Publications, Teachers College, Columbia University, 1952.

Lewin, Kurt, *Resolving Social Conflicts.* Harper & Brothers, 1941.

Martin, William E.; and Stendler, Celia Burns, *Readings in Child Development.* Harcourt, Brace and Company, Inc., 1954.

May, Rollo, *Man's Search for Himself.* W. W. Norton & Company, Inc., 1953.

———— *The Meaning of Anxiety.* The Ronald Press Company, 1950.

Moustakas, Clark E., ed., *The Self:* Explorations in Personal Growth. Harper & Brothers, 1956.

Parkhurst, Helen, *Exploring the Child's World.* Appleton-Century-Crofts, Inc., 1951.

Piaget, Jean, *The Moral Judgment of the Child,* tr. by Marjorie Cabain. The Free Press, 1948.

Roberts, David Everett, *Psychotherapy and a Christian View of Man.* Charles Scribner's Sons, 1950.

Sherrill, Lewis Joseph, *The Gift of Power.* The Macmillan Company, 1955.

———— *Guilt and Redemption* (2d ed.). John Knox Press, 1956.

———— *The Struggle of the Soul.* The Macmillan Company, 1951.

Thorburn, Marjorie, *The Spirit of the Child:* A Study of the Moral and Spiritual Development of Small Children. George Allen & Unwin, Ltd., London, 1946.

Whyte, William H., Jr., *The Organization Man.* Simon and Schuster, Inc., 1956.

Wise, Carroll A., *Psychiatry and the Bible.* Harper & Brothers, 1956.

Yeaxlee, Basil A., *Religion and the Growing Mind.* The Seabury Press, Inc., 1952.

THEOLOGICAL

Aulen, Gustaf, *Christus Victor:* An Historical Study of the Three Main Types of the Idea of the Atonement, tr. by A. G. Hebert. The Macmillan Company, 1951.

———— *The Faith of the Christian Church,* tr. from the 4th Swedish edition by Eric H. Wahlstrom and G. Everett Arden. Muhlenberg Press, 1948.

Bailey, Derrick Sherwin, *The Mystery of Love and Marriage:* A Study in the Theology of Sexual Relation. S.C.M. Press, London, 1952.

Baillie, D. M., *God Was in Christ:* An Essay on Incarnation and Atonement. Charles Scribner's Sons, 1948.

Baillie, John, *And the Life Everlasting.* Charles Scribner's Sons, 1948.

———— *The Belief in Progress.* Charles Scribner's Sons, 1951.

———— *The Idea of Revelation in Recent Thought.* Columbia University Press, 1956.

Barth, Karl, *The Doctrine of Reconciliation (Church Dogmatics,* Vol. IV, part 1), tr. by G. W. Bromiley. Charles Scribner's Sons, 1956.

———— *The Doctrine of the Word of God (Prolegomena to Church Dogmatics) (Church Dogmatics,* Vol. I, part 1), tr. by G. T. Thomson. T. & T. Clark, Edinburgh, 1936.

———— *Prayer According to the Catechisms of the Reformation,* tr. by Sara F. Terrien. The Westminster Press, 1952.

Bartsch, Hans Werner, ed., *Kerygma and Myth:* A Theological Debate, tr. by Reginald H. Fuller. S.P.C.K., London, 1953.

Brunner, Emil, *The Christian Doctrine of Creation and Redemption (Dogmatics,* Vol. II), tr. by Olive Wyon. The Westminster Press, 1952.

_____ *The Christian Doctrine of God (Dogmatics,* Vol. I), tr. by Olive Wyon. The Westminster Press, 1950.

_____ *The Divine-Human Encounter,* tr. by Olive Wyon. The Westminster Press, 1943.

_____ *The Divine Imperative:* A Study in Christian Ethics, tr. by Olive Wyon. The Westminster Press, 1947.

Cairns, David S., *The Image of God in Man.* Philosophical Library, Inc., 1947.

Edwall, Pehr; Hayman, Eric; and Maxwell, William P., eds., *Ways of Worship:* The Report of a Theological Commission of Faith and Order. S.C.M. Press, London, 1951.

Farmer, Herbert H., *The World and God.* Harper & Brothers, 1935.

Ferré, Nels F. S., *The Christian Understanding of God.* Harper & Brothers, 1951.

_____ *Faith and Reason.* Harper & Brothers, 1946.

Flew, R. Nelson, ed., *The Nature of the Church:* Faith and Order. S.C.M. Press, London, 1952.

Galloway, Allan D., *The Cosmic Christ.* Harper & Brothers, 1951.

Hazelton, Roger, *God's Way with Man:* Variations on the Theme of Providence. Abingdon Press, 1956.

Heiler, Friedrich, *Prayer:* A Study in the History and Psychology of Religion, tr. and ed. by Samuel McComb and J. E. Park. Oxford University Press, 1937.

Heim, Karl, *Christian Faith and Natural Science,* tr. by Neville Horton Smith. Harper & Brothers, 1953.

_____ *God Transcendent,* tr. from the 3d German ed. by Edgar P. Dickie. James Nisbet & Co., Ltd., London, 1935.

Homrighausen, Elmer G., *Choose Ye This Day:* A Study of Decision and Commitment in Christian Personality. The Westminster Press, 1943.

Knox, John, *On the Meaning of Christ.* Charles Scribner's Sons, 1947.

Lenker, J. N., ed., *Luther's Catechetical Writings,* Vol. I, *The Law, Faith and Prayer.* Luther Press, 1907.

Mackay, John A., *A Preface to Christian Theology.* The Macmillan Company, 1941.

Nelson, J. Robert, *The Realm of Redemption:* Studies in the Doctrine of the Nature of the Church in Contemporary Protestant Theology. The Epworth Press, London, 1951.

Newbigin, Lesslie, *The Household of God.* Friendship Press, 1954.

Niebuhr, H. Richard, *Christ and Culture*. Harper & Brothers, 1951.

———— *The Meaning of Revelation*. The Macmillan Company, 1946.

Niebuhr, Reinhold, *Faith and History*. Charles Scribner's Sons, 1949.

———— *The Nature and Destiny of Man:* A Christian Interpretation (Vol. I, *Human Nature;* Vol. II, *Human Destiny*). The Gifford Lectures, 1-vol. ed., Charles Scribner's Sons, 1946.

Nygren, Anders, *Agape and Eros,* tr. by A. G. Hebert. 2 vols. S.P.C.K., London, 1932.

———— *The Gospel of God,* tr. by L. J. Trinterud. The Westminster Press, 1951.

Oman, John, *Grace and Personality*. Cambridge University Press, 1931.

Outler, Albert, *Psychotherapy and the Christian Message*. Harper & Brothers, 1954.

Read, David H. C., *The Communication of the Gospel*. S.C.M. Press, London, 1952.

Richardson, Alan, *Christian Apologetics*. Harper & Brothers, 1947.

Tillich, Paul, "Communicating the Gospel," *Union Seminary Quarterly Review,* Vol. VII, No. 4, June, 1952, pp. 3 ff.

———— *Systematic Theology,* Vol. I. University of Chicago Press, 1951.

———— *Existence and the Christ (Systematic Theology,* Vol. II). University of Chicago Press, 1957.

Uhlhorn, Gerhard, *Christian Charity in the Ancient Church*. Charles Scribner's Sons, 1883.

Notes

Chapter 1. The School and the Church

[1] " Schools are public testimony to man's faith in the possibility of control over his own destiny." Childs, John L., *Education and Morals:* An Experimentalist Philosophy of Education. Appleton-Century-Crofts, Inc., 1950, p. 5. Used by permission.

[2] " By religion . . . we mean the religion of Man and the Universe, the cosmic forces gripping mankind and the earth and heaven above." Rugg, Harold Ordway, *Foundations for American Education.* World Book Company, 1947, p. 682. Used by permission.

[3] Madden, Ward, *Religious Values in Education.* Harper & Brothers, 1951, p. 11. Used by permission.

[4] Geren, Paul, *Burma Diary.* Harper & Brothers, 1943, pp. 51 f. Used by permission.

[5] " Norm " is used here to indicate the normative rather than the normal.

[6] Dewey, John, *Democracy and Education:* An Introduction to the Philosophy of Education. The Macmillan Company, 1932, p. 115. Used by permission.

[7] Childs, John L., *op. cit.,* p. 135.

[8] Williams, J. Paul, *The New Education and Religion.* Association Press, 1945, p. 180.

[9] Brubacher, John S., ed., *The Public Schools and Spiritual Values* (Seventh Yearbook of the John Dewey Society). Harper & Brothers, 1944, p. 54. Used by permission.

[10] This point of view may be found in the work of Arthur T. Jersild, *In Search of Self.* Bureau of Publications, Teachers College, Columbia University, 1952, pp. 35 ff.

[11] Karl Barth, for instance, explicates the thesis of " The Word of

God as the Criterion of Dogmatics." He uses the term "the word of God" in a threefold sense: the word of God preached (the proclamation of the gospel), the written Word of God (the Bible), and the revealed Word of God (Jesus Christ). His work is a comprehensive survey of the meaning of the term. See *The Doctrine of the Word of God* (*Prolegomena to Church Dogmatics*) (*Church Dogmatics,* Vol. I, part 1), tr. by G. T. Thomson. T. & T. Clark, Edinburgh, 1936, pp. 98–135, *passim.*

[12] *The Purposes of Education in American Democracy.* National Education Association of the United States and the American Association of School Administrators, 1938, pp. 35 f.

[13] Kilpatrick, William Heard, *Philosophy of Education.* The Macmillan Company, 1951. Professor Kilpatrick lists the psychological bases for values and follows these with a list of twelve elements in "the life good to live," pp. 148–158.

[14] See Wedel, Theodore O., *The Christianity of Main Street.* The Macmillan Company, 1950, pp. 65 f.

[15] See *Moral and Spiritual Values in the Public Schools.* National Education Association of the United States and the American Association of School Administrators, 1951, pp. 31 f.

[16] Kilpatrick, William Heard, *op. cit.,* p. 423.

[17] A good discussion of the subject may be found in Nels F. S. Ferré, *Faith and Reason.* Harper & Brothers, 1946, pp. 47–49.

[18] Paul Tillich defines theological method as the "method of correlation," which "explains the contents of the Christian faith through existential questions and theological answers in mutual interdependence." *Systematic Theology,* (Vol. I). University of Chicago Press, 1951, p. 60.

[19] An interesting illustration may be seen by reading Professor Counts's discussion of the Hebraic-Christian ethic, which he views apart from the theology of the faith. *Education and American Civilization,* Bureau of Publications, Teachers College, Columbia University, 1952, pp. 221 ff.

Chapter 2. THE CONTEXT OF CHRISTIAN EDUCATION

[1] This is illustrated by the literature coming from commissions of the World Council of Churches, such as *The Nature of the Church* (*Faith and Order*), ed. by R. Newton Flew. S.C.M. Press, London, 1952.

2 Knox, John, *On the Meaning of Christ*. Charles Scribner's Sons, 1947, p. 17.

3 Dodd, C. H., *The Apostolic Preaching and Its Developments*. Harper & Brothers, 1936.

4 *Ibid.*, pp. 24–29.

5 *Ibid.*, p. 88.

6 It is, however, set within the framework of myth. See Bartsch, Hans Werner, ed., *Kerygma and Myth*, tr. by Reginald H. Fuller. S.P.C.K., London, 1953. Here Rudolf Bultmann says that in order to be communicated today, the gospel needs to be stripped of its mythological framework. The question is raised: If the myth is removed, will the pure *kērygma* emerge or will there be only an interpretation relative to the theologian's own point of view? Helmut Thielike suggests that myth is the mode *par excellence* for conveying the *kērygma*.

7 Wright, G. Ernest, *God Who Acts*. Henry Regnery Company, 1952, p. 120. Used by permission.

8 Niebuhr, H. Richard, *The Meaning of Revelation*. The Macmillan Company, 1946, p. 135. Used by permission.

9 C. H. Dodd points out that the *kērygma* exerted a controlling influence upon the shaping of the liturgy, and adds that it is perhaps in some parts of the great liturgies of the church that we are still in most direct contact with the original apostolic preaching. *Op. cit.*, p. 74.

10 Luther, Martin, " The Law, Faith and Prayer " (Part 2, " The Apostles' Creed "), from *Luther's Catechetical Writings*, J. N. Lenker, ed. Luther Press, 1907, p. 203.

11 Such references may be found in I Cor. 12:3; Acts 8:37; Heb. 4:14; I John 4:15, which refer to Jesus as the Lord or as the Son of God.

12 Wright, G. Ernest, *op. cit.*, p. 11.

13 Cf. Augustine, " The Lord's Sermon on the Mount," *The Works of the Fathers in Translation*, Vol. 5, tr. by John J. Jepson. The Newman Press, 1948, p. 245.

14 C. H. Dodd sets forth the thesis that the Fourth Gospel was to proclaim the *kērygma* to the Greek-speaking world, whereas the other Gospels were written for the instruction of the Christian community. See *The Interpretation of the Fourth Gospel*, Cambridge University Press, 1953.

15 *The Shorter Catechism of the Westminster Assembly* (Standard ed.). Board of Christian Education of the Presbyterian Church in the U.S.A., 1941. Questions 29 and 30, p. 9.

Chapter 3. THE CONTENT OF CHRISTIAN EDUCATION

1 Heim, Karl, *Christian Faith and Natural Science,* tr. by Neville Horton Smith. Harper & Brothers, 1953, p. 211. Used by permission.
2 Butterfield, Herbert, *Christianity and History.* Charles Scribner's Sons, 1950, p. 7. Used by permission.
3 See the discussion on the Biblical understanding of time as having both a beginning and an end according to the purposes of God, in Cullmann, Oscar, *Christ and Time,* tr. by Floyd V. Filson. The Westminster Press, 1950.
4 A contemporary theologian, Gustaf Aulen, in *Christus Victor,* tr. by A. G. Hebert. The Macmillan Company, 1951, gives an analysis of three widely held theories of the atonement across the centuries. His own leaning is toward that of Irenaeus.
5 A good summary of the meaning of the work of the cross may be found in Baillie, D. M., *God Was in Christ,* pp. 171 f. Charles Scribner's Sons, 1948.
6 Ferré, Nels F. S., *The Christian Understanding of God.* Harper & Brothers, 1951, p. 202. Used by permission.

Chapter 4. PERSONS AND COMMUNICATION

1 Baillie, D. M., op. cit., p. 157. Used by permission.
2 Shapiro, Karl, "Washington Cathedral," in *Midcentury American Poets,* ed. by John Ciardi. Twayne Publishers, Inc., 1953. p. 102. Used by permission.
3 Homans, George Casper, *The Human Group.* Harcourt, Brace and Company, Inc., 1950.
4 Part of this material may be found in Whyte, William H., Jr., *The Organization Man.* Simon and Schuster, Inc., 1956.
5 Sartre, Jean-Paul, *Existentialism and Humanism,* tr. by Philip Mairet. Methuen & Co., Ltd., London, 1948.
6 Marcel, Gabriel, *Being and Having,* tr. by Katharine Farrar. The Dacre Press, London, 1949.
7 Lewin, Kurt, *Resolving Social Conflicts.* Harper & Brothers, 1941.
8 Buber, Martin, *I and Thou,* tr. by Ronald Gregor Smith. T. & T. Clark, Edinburgh, 1937.

9 See Tillich, Paul, *Systematic Theology,* Vol. I, University of Chicago Press, 1951, Part I, pp. 71–157, for a discussion of the problems of knowledge.

10 Heiler, Friedrich, *Prayer:* A Study in the History and Psychology of Religion, tr. and ed. by Samuel McComb and J. E. Park. Oxford University Press, 1937, pp. 356 f.

11 " Petition, therefore, lies at the heart of the awareness of God, and so far from being a primitive immaturity, it is bound up with man's status as a personal being called to find his true maturity in the harmonizing of his will with God's." Farmer, Herbert H., *The World and God.* Harper & Brothers, 1935, p. 137.

Chapter 5. Arriving at Methodology

1 Richardson, Alan, and Schweitzer, W., eds., *Biblical Authority for Today.* The Westminster Press, 1951.

2 Barth, Karl, *op. cit.,* p. 125. The author also warns his readers against dogmatizing the Word: " We do not know the Word of God, whether in its form of proclamation or of Holy Scripture or of revelation, as an essence that exists for itself or could exist only for itself. The sole way we know it is as the Word directed to us, coming home to us " (p. 158).

3 Calvin, John, *The Institutes of the Christian Religion,* tr. by John Allen. The Westminster Press, 1936 ed. (I. vii. 4), p. 90.

4 Within churches that do not practice infant baptism, a function similar to the one here outlined is assigned to the act of dedication of infants.

5 Calvin, John, *op. cit.,* (IV, xv. 22), in Vol. II, p. 602.

6 The denomination's 1957 Assembly changed the official name from " International Convention of Disciples of Christ " to " International Convention of Christian Churches (Disciples of Christ)."

7 Edwall, Pehr; Hayman, Eric; and Maxwell, William P., eds., *Ways of Worship,* a report of the theological commission appointed by the Continuation Committee of the Faith and Order Movement, Part I. S.C.M. Press, London, 1951.

8 Heim, Karl, *God Transcendent,* tr. by Edgar P. Dickie. James Nisbet & Co., Ltd., London, 1935, pp. 156 f. Used by permission.

9 Murray, A. Victor, *Education Into Religion.* Harper & Brothers, 1953, p. 184.

10 In some churches these vows are made at the dedication of the in-

fant, and baptism is given only when the person is able himself to respond to God.

[11] Bushnell, Horace, *Christian Nurture*. Yale University Press, 1950, p. 70. Used by permission.

[12] Homrighausen, Elmer G., " Christian Theology and Christian Education," in *Religious Education,* Nov.–Dec., 1949, p. 353.

[13] Vieth, Paul H., ed., *The Church and Christian Education*. Published for the Cooperative Publishing Association by The Bethany Press, 1947, pp. 66 f. Used by permission.

[14] Mackay, John A., *A Preface to Christian Theology*. The Macmillan Company, 1941, p. 108. Used by permission.

[15] Brunner, Emil, " Nature and Grace," in *Natural Theology,* tr. by Peter Fraenkel. Geoffrey Bles, Ltd., London, 1946, pp. 57 f.

Chapter 6. LIFE-CENTERED METHODS: PARTICIPATION

[1] Thorburn, Marjorie, *The Spirit of the Child*. George Allen & Unwin, Ltd., London, 1946, p. 165. Used by permission.

[2] Shaw, Robert, *J. S. Bach: The Passion According to St. John:* A New Translation Based Upon the King James Version of the Gospel and the Translation of Henry S. Drinker. RCA Victor Division, Radio Corporation of America, n.d. Used by permission.

[3] Rossetti, Christina, *Sing Song*. The Macmillan Company, 1950, p. 114. Used by permission.

[4] *Great Christian Plays,* ed. by Theodore M. Switz and Robert A. Johnston, The Seabury Press, Inc., 1956, contains acting versions in modern English of the Brome *Abraham and Isaac,* the York *Resurrection,* the Digby *Conversion of St. Paul, Everyman,* and *Totentanz.*

[5] Rougemont, Denis de, " Religion and the Mission of the Artist," in *Spiritual Problems in Contemporary Literature,* Stanley Romaine Hopper, ed. Harper & Brothers, 1952, p. 174. Used by permission.

Chapter 7. LIFE-CENTERED METHODS: RECOGNITION
AND COMMUNICATION

[1] This important insight is set forth by Lewis J. Sherrill, in *The Struggle of the Soul*. The Macmillan Company, 1951.

[2] Elmer G. Homrighausen differentiates between " decision " and " commitment." The former means bringing the discussion to an end in favor of one side or another, a separation and differentiation.

It is crucial and final. Commitment is positive; it is a pledge and a surrender, an act and an attitude. One might say that decision precedes commitment. See *Choose Ye This Day*. The Westminster Press, 1943, pp. 59 f.

[3] In some churches the rite of Baptism is deferred until this time.

[4] This is paralleled, to some extent, by the Jewish ceremony of *bar mizvah*, by which the boy becomes a son of the Law.

[5] Parkhurst, Helen, *Exploring the Child's World*. Appleton-Century-Crofts, Inc., 1951. The original radio discs are owned by Union Theological Seminary in New York City. A series of records has been made from them.

[6] *The Confessions of Saint Augustine,* tr. by C. B. Pusey. E. P. Dutton & Co., Inc., 1950, p. 1.

[7] Bushnell, Horace, *op. cit.,* p. 323.

Chapter 8. Focus for the Future

[1] This distinction between the Christian and the world is sometimes noted in the curriculum of "conservative" church groups, usually in moralistic terms.

[2] A recent guide to junior high work, published for the Division of Christian Education of the National Council of the Churches of Christ in the U.S.A. by its Office of Publication and Distribution, New York, n.d., is an excellent aid for leaders, but it has one serious omission: no mention of the Holy Spirit and his work is made anywhere, although the pamphlet is concerned with both faith and work on the junior high level.

[3] The illustrations in the reading books for primary and junior levels have been done this way in the *Christian Faith and Life* curriculum of the Presbyterian Church U.S.A.

[4] The Seabury Series, the curriculum developed by the Department of Christian Education of the National Council of the Protestant Episcopal Church in the U.S.A., The Seabury Press, Inc., 1955 ff., attempts to remedy this defect. Each course begins with the needs of the child and asks, "How is the gospel relevant to these needs?"

[5] Andrews, Dorothy Westlake, *Davie Decides*. The Westminster Press, 1948.

[6] McPherson, Imogene M., *Time for Tommy*. The Westminster Press, 1953.

[7] Perkins, Jeanette E., *Others Call It God*. Harper & Brothers, 1934.

Index

197

BIBLICAL REFERENCES